Morris Goodman, Ph. D.
1 Cypress Street
Maplewood, N. J. 07040

Enhancing Marital Intimacy Through Facilitating Cognitive Self-Disclosure

Enhancing Marital Intimacy Through Facilitating Cognitive Self-Disclosure

By

Edward M. Waring, M.D.

BRUNNER/MAZEL *Publishers* • New York

Library of Congress Cataloging-in-Publication Data

Waring, Edward M., 1944–
  Enhancing marital intimacy through facilitating
cognitive self–disclosure.

  Bibliography: p. 215
  Includes index.
  1. Family psychotherapy. 2. Marital psychotherapy.
3. Self–disclosure. 4. Intimacy (Psychology)
I. Title. [DNLM: 1. Interpersonal Relations.
2. Marital Therapy—methods. 3. Self–Disclosure.
WM 55 W276e]
RC488.5.W36   1987   616.89'156   87-20948
ISBN 0-87630-482-X

Copyright © 1988 by Edward M. Waring

Published by
BRUNNER/MAZEL, INC.
19 Union Square
New York, New York 10003

MANUFACTURED IN THE UNITED STATES OF AMERICA

10 9 8 7 6 5 4 3 2 1

This book is dedicated
to
Sue, Winona, John, and Jennifer

Contents

Preface

This book describes a type of psychotherapy designed to increase marital intimacy, thus improving family functioning. I have spent 10 years studying marital intimacy. I have done research on normal marriages in the general population. I have been involved in therapy with couples who have marital or family problems. The focus of this book is marriage as a psychological relationship. This is, then, a book about the quality of the relationship between a woman and a man in marriage and an approach to helping couples and families who have problems with intimacy.

I wrote this book in a first-person narrative account for several reasons. First, I wish to write in a simple and descriptive style. Second, I have written academic papers on this topic, which are reviewed in the first chapter. I hope to avoid being repetitive in style or content to what has already been published. Third, since the therapy is based on the technique of self-disclosure, I want the style of the book to reflect the therapy. I am making a personal statement. I think that enhancing intimacy through self-disclosure is the most effective, efficient, and humane therapy that I have used to assist distressed families and couples.

I do not believe that this therapy is necessarily the best technique for counseling, but it has been effective for me and some of my students and colleagues. I explain the theory on which this therapy is based to each family or couple I see, describe the research supporting the theory, and demonstrate the technique of self-disclosure in order to negotiate a therapy contract. The book is organized to parallel this process for the reader.

The book has six chapters, covering my experience to date. The first chapter reviews papers that describe the development of the therapy with patients who had a diagnosis of schizophrenia or psychosomatic disorders. The second chapter describes intimacy and its role in family functioning, marriage, and psychological health. The relationship between marital intimacy and self-disclosure is reviewed. Finally, the importance of cognitive self-disclosure is presented.

In the third chapter I describe in general terms how I do a marital intimacy assessment interview. Material from videotapes, audiotapes, and case notes is used so that the reader will have a description of what actually happens in these assessments. I offer ideas about why couples appear to enjoy these interviews.

In the fourth chapter, I describe the technique of therapy. Examples from therapy sessions are presented so that the readers will know what I actually do. The rationale behind the therapy as well as what the couples say and do in therapy is also described.

Chapter 5 presents the results of several outcome studies that I have done either alone or in collaboration with others. Data from some ongoing studies are also reported in order to provide information about efficacy. I hope to communicate the necessity for therapists to objectively evaluate their own assumptions and performance.

Finally, in Chapter 6 I present my ideas about the implications of enhancing intimacy through self-disclosure to the field of family and marital therapy in general. I also describe the areas of lack of knowledge which need to be addressed regarding the effectiveness of this approach.

I hope you enjoy reading my book. I hope the book stimulates you to think about your own marriage and family in a new way. I hope you try this approach with couples and families who come to you for help.

I wish to thank Mrs. M. Davis for her work in bringing this book to publication.

Enhancing
Marital Intimacy
Through Facilitating
Cognitive
Self-Disclosure

1

Enhancing Marital Intimacy Through Cognitive Self-Disclosure

In 1978 a review of family therapy in schizophrenia was published (Waring, 1978). This paper was a result of eight years of experience in working with families in which one or more of the offspring had a diagnosis of schizophrenia. One of the conclusions of that review article was "the parents of schizophrenics show more conflict and disharmony than the parents of other psychiatric patients." In retrospect this conclusion may be incorrect. However, some schizophrenic patients seemed to be sensitive to the quality of their parents' relationship. Relapse in some patients occurred when intimacy between the parents was low.

In my attempts to understand this clinical phenomenon, I happened to read a theory of dyadic interpersonal relationships developed by Schutz (1966). His theory suggested that there are three independent dimensions of interpersonal relationships, which he called inclusion, control, and affection. He suggested that in enduring relationships such as marriage, the affection dimension is the major variable which determines marital satisfaction. This theory was in keeping with the observation of Bowen that "emotional divorce" in the parents of schizophrenics might be related to the course and outcome of the disorder (Bowen, Dysinger, & Basamania, 1959). These two theories suggested that any intervention which decreased the amount of expressed hostility between the parents (or conversely increased supportive statements or closeness) might lead to an improvement in the schizophrenic offspring's symptomatology.

The theory was simple, led to specific action, gave hope, and was capable of verification through treatment success or failure. If I could enhance the parents' intimacy, the course and outcome of the offspring's schizophrenia should improve.

I began to experiment with this approach. The parents were seen alone as a couple. (The schizophrenic offspring was usually seen by an independent psychiatrist for medication and follow-up.) The first session involved an explanation to the couple of the theory of enhancing intimacy to the couple, thus explaining to them why the therapy was being used. The 10 sessions that followed involved:

1. No direct verbal communication between the couple during the session.
2. Each spouse would talk only to me.

3. I discouraged any emotional display during the session.
4. One spouse initiated discussion about his or her thoughts about the disorder and I asked cognitive questions about the problem at hand, including "What is your theory?" I did not ask about feelings but only about the spouses' thinking.
5. When I thought that one spouse had exhausted the topic, I turned to the other spouse and said "What were you thinking while your spouse was talking?" I followed the same procedure throughout the sessions.

The rationale for this type of intervention at the time was:

1. Only the parents are included in the therapy session—other family members are excluded from the emotional system between the parents—thus taking the schizophrenic offspring outside of the couple's emotional system and allowing more cognitive control.
2. The therapist rigidly attempts to stop any emotional interaction between the couple and thus models a different form and method of communication (later to be called cognitive self-disclosure).
3. The therapy was thought to increase the amount of listening done by the spouses, increase the amount of time the spouses spend together, and increase their understanding of one another. This would decrease the use of emotion for control and reduce hostility and criticism leading to an increase in intimacy.

In preliminary experience, this form of family therapy, which was based on an empirical finding of increased

marital disharmony that might affect the course and outcome of schizophrenia, had encouraging results.

In 1980 the first preliminary report of this technique
was published under the term *Cognitive Family Therapy*
(Russell, Russell, & Waring, 1980). This brief description
of the treatment of 22 chaotic, acting-out families in hospital and private practice reported a good outcome for a
method employing cognitive skills.

In this paper, the theory behind the approach was
articulated. The theory stated that in *all* families with
psychopathology, a necessary variable is a "dysfunctional
affective potential" in the marital relationship. This was
conceptualized as a failure of the parents to develop interpersonal intimacy because they did not have the modeling in their own families of origin. The technique of
cognitive self-disclosure attempted to suppress feelings of
criticism and hostility and enhance intimacy in the parents'
marriage. Family functioning then improves and there is
a positive effect on existing psychopathology. The technique allowed for a novel opportunity to "listen" to one's
spouse.

The paper briefly described the method of assessment
which is presented in some detail in Chapter 3. The paper
concluded that this approach provides a viable treatment
choice for immature, chaotic families who frequently terminate treatment prematurely when they are encouraged
to express feelings openly. Their feelings are often primitive
and the technique offers the therapist the opportunity to
avoid being "sucked into the system." Of course, the paper
was only a subjective report of a promising approach which
provided a nonthreatening method.

Later in 1980, Lila Russell and I published a paper
which not only described the technique of using self-

disclosure of cognitive material in more detail but also presented the first objective data suggesting the method might be effective (Waring & Russell, 1980a). The paper was judged by the journal editors as worthy of reproduction in *The International Book of Family Therapy* edited by Kaslow (Waring & Russell, 1982). Some of the outcome data from that study are presented here for the first time.

Self-disclosure was defined as the process of making the private self known to other persons through words. Cognitive self-disclosure refers to revealing one's ideas, attitudes, beliefs, and theories regarding one's relationships.

Cognitive self-disclosure was differentiated from emotional disclosure, which is revealing one's feelings. Self-exposure is disclosing secret or unrevealed behavior that may be detrimental to a relationship. Self-exposure of secrets may be motivated by a wish to distance. Disclosure of negative feelings such as anger often produces distance rather than closeness. *Marital intimacy was thought to be enhanced when the therapist facilitates both spouses to disclose their ideas, attitudes, beliefs, and theories about why the marriage is maladjusted and their thoughts regarding the influence of their parents' marital relationship on their own.*

Intimacy was defined as one dimension of interpersonal relationships within the context of a marriage. Intimacy involves an emotional closeness, a cognitive understanding, behavioral compatibility, and mutual sexual satisfaction.

THE STUDY

The sample consisted of a consecutive series of 11 families in which an individual family member was the presenting patient. However, after individual and family assessment, family therapy was considered the treatment of choice.

These 11 cases represent a subsample of approximately 50 individual referrals for psychiatric outpatient assessment (EMW) or were referred to a general hospital consultation-liaison service in a three-month period (EMW, LR).*

Following the individual and family assessments, 18 families were informed of the nature of the study. The couples were randomly assigned to experienced or inexperienced therapists. Seven families for which family therapy was considered the treatment of choice refused to participate in the study. The reasons given were 1) preference for a specific therapist; 2) objection to completing self-report questionnaires or taping of their sessions; and 3) noncompliance with the suggestion of family therapy. These couples received this self-disclosure approach or other therapy from the authors but are not included in this study sample.

Table 1 (on pp. 10–11) presents the psychiatric diagnosis of the presenting patient and the presenting problem of the family (parents) after the evaluation interview. A spouse was the presenting patient in eight families and a child in three familes (cases 4, 9, and 11). No families were referred specifically for family therapy and only one case (case 9) was referred for marital counseling. Six cases were referred for outpatient psychiatric assessment (cases 1, 3, 4, 5, 8, and 9) and five were referred to the general hospital consultation-liaison service, those presenting with physical symptoms or overdose.

Six cases were diagnosed as having neurotic illnesses, four were diagnosed as having character disorders, and

---

* EMW refers to one of the researchers, a psychiatrist, and LR, a social worker.

one was schizophrenic. Four cases presented as threatened or attempted suicide (cases 1, 3, 5, and 6). All but three cases (cases 3, 4, and 7) had previous psychiatric treatment; previous hospitalization (cases 2, 5, 6, 9, and 10); marital counseling (case 8); and treatment for drug abuse (case 11).

During the course of the 10 weeks of therapy, case 2 received antidepressant medication; case 3 had brief supportive sessions and demanded minor tranquilizers (which were refused) and saw a nonpsychiatrist physician; case 4 was assessed by a child psychoanalyst before and after her parents' therapy; case 9 continued lithium prescribed by another physician; and case 11 received perphenazine and was briefly hospitalized.

In summary, the sample was a difficult heterogeneous treatment group: 1) individuals had moderate to severe psychiatric illness; 2) none were referred for family therapy; and 3) the majority had previous psychiatric treatment and were referred as treatment failures. This heterogeneous group was studied because of the importance of evaluating therapies in ordinary clinical settings, and the results have implications for this approach in difficult patient populations.

All presenting patients received an individual psychiatric interview with one of the researchers (EMW). Assessment interviews were conducted by both researchers. EMW was the therapist for cases 4 and 11, and LR treated cases 1, 5, 7, and 9. The researchers are experienced family therapists.

Case 3 was treated by a nurse, cases 6 and 8 by two social work students, and cases 2 and 10 by the same nurse and a senior psychiatric resident. All had some training in family interviewing but were inexperienced in family therapy.

Table 1
Description of Couples Outcome in Cognitive Family Therapy

Case	Therapist	Number of Sessions	Diagnosis of Identified Patient	Presenting Problem after CFT Assessment	Therapist Rating	Patient Rating	Overall Review
1	E_2	8	Hysterical personality and neurotic depression (F)	1. Psychophysiological symptoms 2. Lack of understanding sexual dysfunction	Unchanged	Worse, but depression and pain better	P+C−ND
2	$I_{1,2}$	10	Psychotic depression (M)	Sexual dysfunction	Improved	"Slightly improved"	P+C+F+
3	I_1	10	Hysterical personality disorder (F)	1. Poor communication 2. Lack of intimacy	Unchanged	Worse	P±C−F+
4	E_1	10	Daughter (age 7) nightmares	Marital dysfunction	Improved	Improved	P+C+F+
5	E_2	10	Neurotic depression (M)	1. Lack of closeness 2. Emotional divorce	Improved	"Much improved"	P+C+ND

6	I_3	10	Hysterical personality disorder (F)	Lack of understanding	Unchanged	Unchanged	P±C±F+
7	E_2	10	Hysterical personality disorder (F)	Sexual dysfunction	Improved	Improved	ND C±F+
8	I_4	10	Hysterical personality disorder (F)	1. Lack of closeness 2. Lack of understanding	Unchanged	"Very slightly improved"	P+C±F±
9	E_2	8	Obsessive-compulsive son (homosexual) (M)	Sexual concerns	Unchanged	—	P+C+F+
10	$I_{1,2}$	10	Neurotic depression (F)	Lack of closeness	Improved	"Beautiful" improved	P+C+F+
11	E_1	10	Son (schizophrenic)	Lack of intimacy	Improved	Unchanged	P+C±F+
					I	80%	45%	88%
					U	20%	40%	12%

Key: E_1 = experienced psychiatrist; E_2 = experienced social worker; I_1 = inexperienced nurse; I_2 = inexperienced resident; I_3 = inexperienced social worker student; I_4 = inexperienced student; C = couple; F = family (includes children, in-laws, family of origin); + = improved; − = worse; ± = unchanged; ND = no data; I = improved; U = unimproved; (F) = female; (M) = male.

The training of the nurse, social work students, and resident was of particular importance. They all attended a weekly family therapy seminar. The four "student" therapists attended a one-day workshop to train them in the technique of enhancing marital intimacy. This consisted of an introductory lecture, viewing videotapes of both assessment interviews and a cognitive self-disclosure therapy session, and role playing of assessment and therapy. They then received one hour of supervision from one of the authors for each hour of therapy.

Supervision, by audiotape, focused on whether they were doing therapy in a standardized fashion as previously described and focused on why they were not using cognitive self-disclosure if this was the case. The students uniformly had difficulty initially with the "cognitive response" approach and reacted to behavior and feeling. In all cases the students gradually began to use self-disclosure in a standardized way and the need for supervision decreased. Thus the supervision process ensured that all therapists were employing the same technique.

It must be emphasized that, although a uniformity and standardization of the technique was obtained through audiotaping and supervision of the sessions, therapist personality variables and nonspecific treatment factors were not controlled. In fact, the students were encouraged through their personality, interpersonal style, and "use of self" outside of the therapy sessions to do whatever was necessary to facilitate the families continuing the sessions.

Following the assessment interview, specific and explicit explanation of theory, therapy, and treatment contract was completed and an informed consent was obtained. The couples were then randomly assigned to one of six therapists who was next on the therapy list if they had available time. The 11 couples were requested to complete the following self-report questionnaires: General Health Questionnaire (Goldberg, 1972); Zung Depression Scale (Zung, 1963); Locke–Wallace Marital Adjustment (Locke & Wallace, 1959); Family Environment Scale (Moos & Moos, 1976); and Fundamental Interpersonal Relations Orientation-Behavior (Schutz, 1966), prior to treatment and at termination.

The General Health Questionnaire is a 60-item self-report questionnaire for the detection of nonpsychotic emotional illness (Goldberg, 1972). A symptom score greater than 12 suggests the possibility of neurotic or psychophysiological illness.

The Zung Depression Scale is a standardized self-report questionnaire which measures depressive symptoms (Zung, 1963). The Locke–Wallace is a 16-item self-report questionnaire which measures marital adjustment (Locke & Wallace, 1959).

The Family Environment Scale (FES) assesses the social climates of all types of families (Moos & Moos, 1976). In this study we focused on the measurement and description of 1) the interpersonal relationships among family members: cohesion, expressiveness, and conflict; and 2) system maintenance dimensions: organization and control (see the appendix for definitions).

The Fundamental Interpersonal Relations Orientation-Behavior (FIRO-B) is a self-report questionnaire measuring inclusion, control, and affection (Schutz, 1966). In this study we focused only on affective compatibility, which Schutz suggests is most important in enduring relationships such as marriage, and conceptually it was related to intimacy. In general, affection behavior refers to close personal emotional feelings between two people. Reciprocal

Compatibility (rK) refers to the degree to which husband and wife reciprocally satisfy each other's behavior preferences for affection. Originator Compatibility (oK) is based more directly in the originate–receive axis. If both partners wish to receive, the sign will be negative (−). Interchange Compatibility (xK) refers to the mutual expression of affection. The interpretation of xK is analogous to rK and oK; the smaller the value, the greater the compatibility.

The following hypotheses were made with reference to the 11 couples who received this therapy: 1) GHQ scores of neurotic symptoms would decrease; 2) Zung depression scores would decrease; 3) LWMA scores would increase; 4) cohesion, expressiveness, organization, and control would increase, and conflict decrease, in the FES; and 5) affection compatibility would increase (representing a decrease in FIRO-B scores).

As well as the objective tests, three other outcome measures were utilized: 1) therapist subjective rating of improved, unchanged, or worse at 10 weeks; 2) patient subjective rating of improvement at one- to three-month follow-up; and 3) and *overall rating* by the authors (EMW and LR) of identified patient *(P)*, the married couple *(C)*, and the family *(F)*, based on subjective reports of patient and therapist, clinical case notes, objective tests taken individually, and information from referral source.

Our final hypothesis was the prediction of no difference between experienced and inexperienced therapists. An exploratory, descriptive attempt was made to identify characteristics of those families who benefited most or least from this therapy approach.

RESULTS

Therapist Ratings

The therapists rated six cases as improved and five cases as unchanged with no cases reported as worse. If one adds to the six improved the one case whose principals considered themselves improved despite the therapist rating them as unchanged, the rate of 64% approximates the general results of all psychotherapy research and uncontrolled family therapy outcome studies (Gurman & Kniskern, 1975; Wells & Dezen, 1978).

Patient Ratings

Six families rated themselves improved (60%), two rated themselves unchanged, two worse but in one of these cases the patient reported the presenting problems (pain and depression) were improved, and one case had no rating. The two cases who evaluated themselves as worse were seen as unchanged by their therapist, and there was a discrepancy in two other cases between therapist and patient ratings, one in each direction.

Overall Ratings

The difficulties with subjective ratings have been discussed frequently in the literature but do provide the clinical reality of evaluation for therapist and patients. The overall ratings (EMW and LR) provide a perspective of the different outcome variables evaluated. In case 1, the presenting symptoms of pain and depression were improved, but a chronic marital maladjustment previously denied was overt and unresolved at termination. The couple terminated two sessions early because they recognized their maladjustment and were uncertain if they wished to separate or to stay together. Case 2 presented improved depression, marital adjustment, and family functioning, but a specific sexual dysfunction was unchanged. Case 3 presented with suicidal threats, which had diminished, but the overt marital maladjustment was unresolved and separation was being considered. In case 4, the child's symptoms disappeared and the couple felt closer than before. Case 5 resulted in depression improvement and marital adjustment. Case 6 showed improvement in depression and decreased suicidal risk but marital maladjustment was unresolved. Case 7 showed improvement in behavior, sexuality, and marital adjustment. Case 8 showed improved understanding and communication, but an unresolved battle for control—the result of a forced marriage—remained. Case 9 revealed chronic covert marital maladjustment and sexual problems, but increased understanding and less concern with their homosexual son, resulting in premature termination as they felt they received what they wanted. Case 10 showed improvement in symptoms and relationship. Case 11 improved understanding and communication in marriage, the son was symptom-free while on phenothiazines, out of hospital, living on his own, and attending an outpatient group, but previously covert marital maladjustment was now overt.

In summary, in all but two cases (3 and 6) the presenting problem or symptoms were clearly improved, 80% symptomatic improvement with no worsening in cases 3 and 6. Obviously, the families rated as unchanged or worse were couples with covert marital maladjustment which was now overt and largely unresolved, although oddly enough, family functioning was improved in families rated as worse or unchanged because of overt marital maladjustment.

Table 2 presents the results of analysis of difference in the GHQ, Zung, and LWMA before and after therapy. The GHQ scores were reduced to the normal range below the score of 12, which is the cutoff point for high probability in cases of nonpsychotic emotional illness (Goldberg, 1972). The reduction of the neurotic symptom scores approached statistical significance even in this small sample. As predicted, there was a reduction in depression scores and an increase in marital adjustment, but these were not statistically significant.

Table 3 presents the relationship and system maintenance scores from the FES. As predicted, cohesion, expressiveness, control, and organization increased, and conflict was reduced, the latter again approaching statistical significance in a small sample.

Table 2
Changes in Symptom Scores and Marital Adjustment Before and After Therapy

Test	Number of Individuals	Pretest	Posttest	T	Significance
GHQ	14	17.6	7.6	1.99	$p<.06$*
ZUNG	14	40.09	38.9	.81	$p<.43$
LWMA	8 (couples)	96.8	105.8	$-.76$	$p<.47$

* Score of >12 indicates a case of nonpsychotic emotional illness on GHQ.

Table 4 presents the results of compatibility scores on the affection dimension of FIRO-B. An interesting observation supporting previous research is the (−) sign for oK, suggesting couples with psychiatric difficulties prefer to receive affection rather than give affection. The study shows that all types of compatibility improved (i.e., approached zero), but none reached statistical significance.

In summary, although none of the objective parameters reached traditionally accepted levels of significance ($p <$

Table 3

Changes in Family Environment Before and After Therapy

Test	Number of Couples	Pretest	Posttest	T	Significance
COH	8	6.87	7.13	−.39	$p>.71$
EX	8	5.12	5.50	−.81	$p>.44$
CON	8	4.63	3.50	2.18	$p>.06$
ORG	8	5.12	5.37	−.55	$p>.59$
CTL	8	5.25	5.75	−1.53	$p>.17$

Table 4

Changes in Compatibility Scores Before and After Therapy

Compatibility	Number of Couples	Pretest	Posttest	T	Significance
rK aff	7	+4.8	+3.1	−1.14	$p>.28$
oK aff	7	−4.8	−3.1	−1.14	$p>.28$
xK aff	7	1.7	1.4	.07	$p>.94$

.05), the fact that all parameters improved in the expected direction, and that two approached significance in a small sample, suggested that further study of this approach was warranted.

The sample size was too small to allow statistical comparison of experienced versus inexperienced therapists. According to therapist ratings, the experienced therapists rated 66% as improved as compared to 40% for the inexperienced therapists. However, there was no difference in the patients' ratings, with a 60% improvement rate in both groups, and each had a patient who rated himself or herself as worse. In the overall ratings, the inexperienced therapists had the only two cases who did not improve symptomatically, but there was no apparent difference in couple or family outcome and the experienced therapists had all the missed sessions.

One important observation was about the two cases who considered themselves worse at follow-up, supporting previous research which suggests that psychotherapy can make patients worse, and this must be assessed in outcome research (Strupp, Hadley, & Gomes-Schwartz, 1977). It is obvious that patients with neurotic symptoms without severe character disorder do best with this therapy and this is hardly surprising. Although the cases who reported themselves worse at follow-up were diagnosed as hysterical personality disorders, other cases with this diagnosis did well.

On closer examination we found that in the two cases reported as worse, physical symptoms had masked chronic, covert marital maladjustment. The therapy made the marital maladjustment overt but was unable to provide satisfactory resolution in 10 sessions. This suggests either that the therapy was contraindicated in these cases, or that longer treatment was necessary. However, our clinical experience has shown that at 6- to 12-month follow-up, most cases with covert marital maladjustment made overt with this approach have found a resolution and evaluate the therapy most favorably. Obviously, more research is necessary to resolve this issue—these two cases were also identifiable at the onset with both partners complaining of a lack of understanding, an interesting observation in terms of the theoretical importance of cognitive self-disclosure.

This uncontrolled clinical outcome study of a therapy designed to enhance marital intimacy through cognitive self-disclosure in the treatment of moderate to severe psychiatric illness suggested that further evaluation of this technique was indicated.

The most interesting finding in the study was treatment compliance. In this study, the families attended 106 of a possible 110 sessions, which is a remarkable compliance rate supporting our previous clinical experience of high compliance rates following assessment. Possible reasons for this, particularly in a sample not referred for family therapy, included 1) short-term approach; 2) specific, explicit treatment contract; 3) explicit theory; 4) nonthreatening nature of sessions; and 5) therapist enthusiasm.

A second finding in the study is the absence of difference in outcome or compliance between experienced and inexperienced therapists, as can be observed in Table 1. The training period was extremely short, the amount of supervision high, but once the trainees began to actually do therapy the time for supervision decreased. The high compliance rate and short training of inexperienced therapists are stimulating aspects of this study.

Despite limitations in the research design, several conclusions regarding the therapy appeared supportable from this study. Neurotic symptomatology was improved in 80% of the cases, which is above usually reported spontaneous improvement rates for neurosis. In 45% of these cases the therapy also produced improvement in marital adjustment and an 88% improvement in family functioning. In the other 55% covert marital maladjustment became overt during the course of this therapy and in some cases could not be resolved in the 10 sessions of this approach of self-disclosure, if it could be resolved at all. The two cases who evaluated their experience with this therapy as worse at follow-up were women with hysterical personality disorders who had physical symptoms and threatened suicide, and who recognized with their husbands their profound marital maladjustment during therapy. In both cases, understanding why their interpersonal relationships were maladjusted did not lead to behavioral change, although it did produce symptomatic improvement.

This promising study was followed by a clinical paper which described intimacy, self-disclosure, and cognitive self-disclosure in more detail (Waring, 1981). This paper also reviewed psychiatric literature which suggested a relationship between lack of intimacy and emotional disorder. Henderson (1980) had reviewed data which were at least consistent with, but cannot yet prove, the hypothesis that a deficiency in social bonds is a cause of nonpsychotic emotional illness. He suggested these deficiencies in social bonds may involve both close, affectionate bonds and more diffuse social relationships. Hinde (1978) argued that we must search for a science of interpersonal relationships within the context of social bond theory. Intimacy is one dimension of close, affectionate bonds in interpersonal relationships which merits increased investigation.

Berman and Lief (1975) described marital relationships in terms of three interpersonal variables: boundary, power, and intimacy. Feldman (1979) described a variety of unconscious conflicts causing both failure to develop intimacy and fear of losing intimacy resulting in a pattern of repetitive conflict and conciliation. Horowitz (1979) suggested that the most common interpersonal factor identified by patients as the reason they sought outpatient psychotherapy is failure to develop intimacy. Brown, Brolchain, and Harris (1975) demonstrated that the absence of a "close, confiding relationship" is one of four vulnerability factors in the development of depression in women under adverse circumstances. Henderson et al. (1980) in a study on neurosis in an urban population demonstrated that neurosis is mainly associated with deficiency in close attachment, although more diffuse social bonds also play a role. Hames and Waring (1979) demonstrated a significant relationship in psychiatric patients between a lack of marital intimacy as measured by self-report questionnaire and severity of nonpsychotic emotional illness. In a second study in the general population, Waring et al. (1981a) demonstrated that lack of marital intimacy as measured by structured interview is associated with the prevalence of nonpsychotic emotional illness and psychiatric help-seeking. Vaillant (1978) suggested that capacity for maintaining intimacy in close adult relationships is a determinant of adult male psychological health. Intimacy may be the interpersonal factor which most determines marital maladjustment (Waring, 1980). Lewis et al. (1976) reveal that opportunities for intimacy are a determinant of optimal family functioning. Weissman and Paykel (1974), Speck and Rueveni

(1969), and Pattison (1977) suggest that therapy for non-psychotic emotional illness should focus, at least in part, on reconnecting such deficient social bonds.

In summary, the assumption that an empirical intervention which facilitates marital intimacy might be expected to improve marital adjustment and reduce symptoms of nonpsychotic emotional illness appeared to merit further evaluation.

WHAT IS MARITAL INTIMACY?

In a series of studies we had developed an operational definition of intimacy as "a multifaceted interpersonal dimension which describes the quality of a marital relationship at a point in time" (Waring et al., 1981b). Intimacy is a composite of 1) affection—the degree to which feelings of emotional closeness are expressed by the couple; 2) expressiveness—the degree to which thoughts, beliefs, attitudes, and feelings are communicated within the marriage; 3) compatibility—the degree to which the couple is able to work and play together comfortably; 4) cohesion—a commitment to the marriage; 5) sexuality—the degree to which sexual needs are communicated and fulfilled; 6) conflict resolution—the ease with which differences of opinion are resolved; 7) autonomy—the couple's degree of positive connectedness to family and friends; and 8) identity—the couple's level of self-confidence and self-esteem. Other operational definitions of intimacy are also available (Schaefer & Olson, 1981).

WHAT IS SELF-DISCLOSURE?

Jourard and Sasoko (1958) were the first to systematically study the phenomenon of self-disclosure which they believed was a "symptom of health" and a "means to interpersonal effectiveness." Chelune (1978) defines self-disclosure as "a process of making ourselves known to other persons by verbally revealing personal information." Self-disclosure can be classified as: 1) expression of emotion; 2) expression of need; 3) expression of thought, attitudes, beliefs, and fantasy; and 4) self-awareness. The latter two are defined here as "cognitive self-disclosure."

Now let us return to our operational definition of intimacy. Jourard and Sasoko (1958) demonstrated that the most consistent personal disclosures occurred in the marital relationship. Waterman (1980) reviewed studies which demonstrate a positive relationship between amount of self-disclosure and marital adjustment. Several authors have suggested that self-disclosure may be an important determinant of a couple's level of intimacy (Schaefer & Olson, 1981; Waring & Russell, 1980a). Waring and Chelune (1983) empirically demonstrated that self-disclosure is a significant determinant of the rated levels of expressiveness, compatibility, identity, and intimacy behavior, four of the eight factors which define level of intimacy. Thus self-disclosure determines 50% of the variance of rated level of intimacy in married couples.

Cognitive Self-Disclosure

Cognitive self-disclosure refers to the process of making ourselves known to others by verbally revealing personal thoughts, beliefs, attitudes, and assumptions, as well as developing self-awareness. Waring et al. (1980) found that cognitive self-disclosure was thought by couples in the general population to be the primary determinant of intimacy. This finding supported an earlier observation by Grinker (1967) that cognitive knowledge or "knowing" one's partner may be a primary determinant of a couple's level of intimacy. Is there evidence to support this relationship? Levinger and Senn (1967) demonstrated that there is more disclosure of unpleasant feelings, affective self-disclosure of a negative quality, in unsatisfied couples—disclosure of negative feelings produces distance and is characteristic of disturbed families. Murstein (1974) suggests that a major problem in marriage is a failure to disclose attitudes, values, and beliefs during courtship, which results in a lack of cognitive information that could prevent choices in which conflicting value systems prevent closeness.

Sullivan (1953) was the first to suggest the therapeutic value of self-disclosure. Fromm (1955) was the first to recognize that self-disclosure could decrease the phenomenological distance between self and others. Burke, Weir, and Duwors (1979) suggested that self-disclosure can be facilitated through training or psychotherapy.

Self-disclosure is facilitated when the material disclosed is perceived as appropriate in the context of the relationship and the listener is perceived as nurturant and supportive, and also willing to disclose in a reciprocal pattern. Finally, the longer an individual speaks on topics regarding self, the more intimate the disclosures become.

The second assumption is that, since self-disclosure has been demonstrated to be an important determinant of intimacy, any technique that alters the amounts of self-disclosure will influence the level of intimacy. Finally, cognitive self-disclosure is facilitated in a structured situation where the material disclosed is relevant and the listener is perceived as nurturant and willing to disclose reciprocally.

The paper goes on to describe couples' experience with this therapy. Both spouses often perceive one of their parents as being more responsible for the unhappiness in the parental generation. Cognitive restructuring results in a shift to a more balanced understanding of the interactive component of their parents' relationships and a growing awareness that the parent who was held less responsible for the difficulty shared with the offspring the same traits which he or she was unable to recognize and accept. This is a common phenomenon in the successfully treated couple. The increased contact with the family of origin for information is also characteristic of successfully treated couples.

Intriguing questions are: Why is this therapeutic approach effective? Can this therapy help answer the question of whether deficiencies of marital intimacy as one specific type of social bond play a causative role in nonpsychotic emotional illness? Is the therapy effective due to the process of facilitating cognitive self-disclosure, as our theory suggests, or some other phenomenon, such as modeling, cognitive restructuring, or nonspecific psychotherapy factors (e.g., the restoration of morale)? Is lack of cognitive self-disclosure the common factor which explains the relationship between deficient marital intimacy and nonpsychotic emotional illness?

To answer the question of whether deficiencies in marital intimacy play a causative role in nonpsychotic emotional illness, a different order of question must be asked. A research design must be constructed, such as, Does a group of married neurotic depressive women matched for adverse circumstances and severity of symptoms show greater symptomatic improvement in level of marital intimacy if treated with antidepressants or cognitive self-disclosure? This type of research design allows for the possibility that neurosis is a causative factor in deficient marital intimacy.

The question of why the self-disclosure therapy is effective can be answered only by a component analysis of the relationship of the amount of cognitive self-disclosure in the sessions and its variance with outcome and/or comparison with other components such as self-disclosure of feelings as opposed to thoughts, or varying the content of the self-disclosure. The question of whether the *process* of facilitating cognitive self-disclosure or the *content* of the disclosures resulting in cognitive restructuring is therapeutic remains to be answered.

Some preliminary comments about clinical experience with facilitating cognitive self-disclosure and its effect on intimacy were possible. Couples who both objectively and subjectively derive the greatest benefit spend more time disclosing about the past than the present, and about their parents' marriages rather than about their own. The greater the understanding of their own responsibility for mate selection of a spouse with certain qualities or traits (which decreases the amount of projection onto the spouse), the greater the improvement. The greater the other spouse can facilitate cognitive restructuring with objective data about his or her own parents' relationship, the greater the improvement.

The couples articulate that understanding their spouse, learning to be better listeners without reacting defensively or emotionally, and learning about their psychological roots all play a role in improving their closeness. The ability to enjoy listening to their parents describe their own marriages is the greatest single predictor of positive outcome.

Finally, the technique has impressed on this observer that the experience and observation of one's parents' level of intimacy has a more obvious influence on developing a parallel repetitive pattern in the current marital relationship than the quality of the affectionate bond between the child and either parent (Waring et al., 1980). In fact, the spouse in a maladjusted marriage would appear to be acting as a "misguided marital counselor," emotionally reacting and attempting to change behaviors of his or her mate, which on examination turn out to be the behaviors of the parent who was perceived to be the cause of the parents' lack of intimacy.

Two papers go on to describe the use of the technique of enhancing intimacy through facilitating cognitive self-disclosure in patients with psychosomatic symptoms (Waring, 1980, 1983). Psychosomatically ill patients with diagnosis of chronic pain, morbid obesity, and some with myocardial infarction often differ in their marital adjustment and structure from nonpatient controls. As perceived by the patient as well as the spouse, marital adjustment is about the same as adjustment perceived by nonpatient couples, measured on the Locke–Wallace Marital Adjustment Scale (Locke & Wallace, 1959). The marriages of patients with psychosomatic illness, however, are characterized by specific incompatibilities, primarily in the area of interpersonal intimacy: one spouse does not wish to discuss personal matters; the couple does not share feelings or engage in cognitive self-disclosure; there is a lack of family cohesion as measured by the Family Environment Scale (Moos & Moos, 1976); there is a profound lack of closeness or intimacy.

The inability to discuss personal matters, private thoughts, fantasy, and attitudes has been referred to as "alexithymia" in the psychosomatic literature (Sifneos, 1975). Difficulty in discussing their feelings in their interpersonal relationships in psychological terms is a specific feature of couples in which one has a psychosomatic illness. One spouse's psychosomatic symptoms have crucial meaning for the psychodynamics of the other spouse. Psychosomatic symptoms also affect the general communication of personal suffering or distress within the marital relationship.

Couples in which one spouse has a psychosomatic illness also have incompatibilities in interpersonal areas other than intimacy. For instance, such a spouse prefers to select his or her own company; this is seen as an incompatibility in the area of inclusion as measured by the Fundamental Interpersonal Relations Orientation-Behavior test (Schutz, 1966). Further, each spouse wants to be told what to do and neither partner will take the initiative; this denotes a passive conflict regarding control.

Family structures of patients with psychosomatic illness also demonstrate enmeshment and isolation from extrafamilial social and interpersonal contact. They also evidence a lack of problem-solving skills, which may be related to the absence of cognitive self-disclosure or alexithymia.

Although I have reviewed a significant correlation between patients with chronic physical symptoms of obscure etiology and deficiencies of interpersonal intimacy in their marriages and noted that significant statistical correlations do not explain cause and effect relationships, there is no evidence that deficient intimacy or lack of cognitive self-disclosure predisposes an individual to psychosomatic illness. Some support for lack of intimacy as a precipitating or perpetuating variable in abnormal illness is available (Waring et al., 1981a). Thus marital assessment and/or therapy can only be considered an adjunct to empirical effects at symptomatic treatment.

I will now discuss the implications of this research to the clinician responsible for managing such patients in these three distinct areas: 1) the engagement of the spouse in the evaluation process, 2) the evaluation process itself, and 3) specific marital therapy.

Although in the minds of most psychosomatic patients and their spouses the relationship of their marriage to the presence of physical symptoms seems remote, most spouses are able to recognize that they have "suffered" with the symptoms of the spouse who has chronic physical symptoms of obscure etiology. Thus a simple statement to the spouse, such as "In my experience most people suffer with the physical symptoms of their spouse," may encourage the spouse to ventilate feelings of helplessness and, most commonly, dysphoria. Often there is an underlying resentment toward the spouse with the physical symptoms, but my experience has been that attempts to allow ventilation or recognition of such feelings lead to disengagement and avoidance of evaluation by the spouse and should be left until much later in the therapeutic management of the patient.

The evaluation of the couple's relationship in greater depth is facilitated by the ventilation discussed above. I then prepare a comprehensive marital history of the couple, with their permission, focusing on their perceptions and observations of their parents' marriage as well as how they met, their courtship, engagement, honeymoon, and a developmental history of their family up to the present. A specific focus is placed on their cognitive theories of why the chronic symptoms have persisted for so long.

In general, in the initial evaluation with these couples, I avoid an evaluation of their current relationship because, as suggested by the research, a couple often perceives the marriage to be well adjusted, usually because of an absence of arguments or overt conflict in their relationships. Thus more pertinent information about their level of intimacy and self-disclosure and specific deficiencies in these areas are obtained by the historical method rather than a confrontation, which again in my experience leads couples to disengagement and the absence of a therapy contract.

Finally, if the patient fails to show symptomatic improvement with a variety of therapeutic interventions, I will meet with the couple for a second interview. At that time I suggest directly to them that we have found that couples who suffer with chronic physical symptoms of obscure etiology often are not as close as they wish they were and have difficulties in terms of sharing their private ideas, assumptions, beliefs, and values about their relationship. I continue to find it surprising that many couples accept the proposition that these factors may play a role in perpetuating such symptoms and are willing to participate in some sessions to increase their level of intimacy by facilitating cognitive self-disclosure.

Thus these couples embark on a structured technique of self-disclosure in a reciprocal manner in the presence of a supportive listener. There then appears to be some evidence that this facilitates the couple's level of intimacy and reduces abnormal illness behavior and the sick role.

In summary, the knowledge that the spouses of patients with chronic physical symptoms of obscure etiology experience considerable dysphoria encourages an engagement process in which the spouse is involved in a comprehensive evaluation of the marital relationship. Moreover, knowledge that the couple perceives their marital adjustment as satisfactory allows the avoidance of unnecessary confrontations in the initial evaluation interview which would undermine any future therapeutic potential with the couple. Finally, in a significant proportion of cases, ventilation of the dysphoria and the nonstressful nature of the initial evaluation permit the therapist to explain the evidence regarding intimacy and self-disclosure to the couple. In most cases this can lead to the use of brief cognitive self-disclosure as an adjunctive and clinically effective form of marital therapy.

Because the psychosomatically ill patient has difficulties in experiencing and expressing feelings produced by a growing awareness of unconscious conflicts that may play a part in the predisposition to his illness or by the confrontation of interpersonal difficulties, the patient is not likely to respond well to either insight-oriented individual therapy or marital or family counseling in which feeling is stimulated or uncovered. Thus a therapy such as brief cognitive self-disclosure that focuses on the interpersonal, deals with the psychological strengths and motivations of the spouse, as well as the patient, concentrates on facilitating the expression of cognitive material, and suppresses affect has several advantages in treating the psychosomatically ill patient. First, I have observed that these couples are willing to accept that their difficulties in cognitive self-disclosure may perpetuate their physical symptoms. Second, the spouses of these patients are highly motivated to listen to their spouses in the therapeutic situation and can act as facilitating models. Finally, the increased intimacy that develops allows the couples to give up physical symptoms as an attempt to communicate and allow them to understand and problem solve any marital maladjustment.

A clinical trial of enhancing intimacy in a specific psychosomatic disorder utilizing random assignment and a control therapy is certainly indicated.

The final paper published on this approach brings us back to the starting point of the observation of schizophrenic patients and their parents' marriages. The assumption that the emotional relationship of the marital coalition has a profound influence on family functioning and the individual psychological development of children in the family is not new or startling (Ackerman, 1958; Bowen, 1960; Minuchin, 1974; Wesley & Epstein, 1969). However, family interactional research which has attempted to understand the etiology of schizophrenia demonstrates that parents are characterized by greater maladjustment, hostility, and criticism of the offspring, particularly in the presence of the schizophrenic patient (Jacob, 1975; Sharan, 1966). In a recent review of family therapy in the treatment of schizophrenia, empirical evidence was presented which suggests that the parents' marriages often are characterized by conflict and disharmony as well as abnormal patterns of communication (Waring, 1978). Leff (1978) describes the quality of this marital conflict as the absence of affection, warmth, and interest, which he believes may be related to "expressed emotion" toward the schizophrenic patient which may be a major factor in precipitating rehospitalization.

Leff's clinical observations may be describing a failure of the marital coalition to develop intimacy in the spouses' interpersonal relationships. Wynne, Toohey, and Doane (1979) have also described specific communication difficulties that occur in the marriages of schizophrenic offspring, which again may be related to inappropriate self-disclosure.

The 10 schizophrenic patients in this study were all between the ages of 18 and 28 and never previously hospitalized for schizophrenia. There were six males and four females. They were consecutive referrals to the author as outpatients or general hospital consultations with intact families over a two-year period.

The parents of all 10 patients were married and living together and attended this therapy assessment interview. One family refused to participate in the self-disclosure sessions after the theory and therapy were explained to them. This family believed that their son's illness was genetic in etiology, although they denied a family history of schizophrenia and they refused to participate. A second family terminated after a third session, refusing to self-disclose regarding the wife's sexual frigidity present from the beginning of the marriage. The case to be presented terminated by mutual consent with the therapist after five sessions because they believed they understood their lack of intimacy and there were realistic travel problems. In summary, the couples missed a total of 17 out of a possible 100 therapy hours.

The clinical characteristics of the group who completed both assessment and a course of 10 sessions are:

1. A reactive or schizophreniform psychosis in the identified patient.
2. Siblings of schizophrenics clearly identify a parental dysfunction in the initial interview and have plausible cognitive explanations of dysfunction.
3. "Psychological flexibility" in the parents.

4. Depressive illness in the mother and depressive symptoms during the course of therapy.
5. The identified schizophrenic patient usually is younger,
   in the 16 to 20 age group.
6. The parents accept the theory that their interpersonal
   interaction may have an influence on their child's behavior.

The families who did not complete therapy or complete
the assessment interview show the opposite clinical variables (process schizophrenia; sibling mystification; parental
psychological inflexibility), with the father showing paranoid features, and the fathers are primarily responsible
for refusal to complete or initiate the self-disclosure sessions. The stated reasons are usually inability to make time
for sessions, disagreement with the theory presented, and
unwillingness to share private thoughts. It must be emphasized that these families have *not* completed 10 sessions
of this therapeutic approach.

The seven schizophrenic offspring whose parents completed this therapy are not "cured" but are functioning
socially with outpatient follow-up. The two patients whose
families refused therapy have had prolonged institutional
care. Only two of the eight who completed 10 sessions
have required rehospitalization in a three-year follow-up.
One patient has had two short (less than two weeks)
readmissions to the general hospital and one patient has
had one short readmission. Four of the eight have never
been on phenothiazine medication while four continue on
phenothiazine dosage (Stelazine less than 20 milligrams
daily) as outpatients.

Several interesting clinical observations regarding the
marriages of parents who have a schizophrenic offspring

are revealed. The couples perceive their marriages as adjusted but on closer evaluation lack of interpersonal intimacy and the absence of self-disclosure are revealed. The clinical observation merits empirical evaluation but is similar to our findings in the marriages of patients with chronic physical symptoms of obscure etiology (Waring & Russell, 1980b). The couples not only attempt to maintain a social facade of marital adjustment but deny specific incompatibilities on superficial questioning. The process of cognitive self-disclosure allows specific differences of opinion and assumptions which have produced distance to be revealed without emotional turmoil or negative consequences.

A second observation is that the context of the offspring's delusions often reveals ideas and assumptions held by the parents as nondisclosed reasons for their lack of marital intimacy (Ackerman, 1958). The questions that deserve further study are how parental assumptions which are kept private can be transmitted to the content of an offspring's delusional system and whether this is a general phenomenon.

Finally, a couple who disguise and distort their lack of marital intimacy, as do couples in this study, present their offspring for help at the developmental stage of development of intimacy for the offspring. A major clinical feature of adolescent onset schizophrenia is the overt expression of rejecting intimacy with members of the opposite sex. The process of cognitive self-disclosure with these couples leads to a reported increase in their closeness with a resultant reduction of tension in the home with less frequently expressed concern about the schizophrenic offspring.

Obviously, these clinical observations are preliminary and may be a result of observer bias. However, they are presented in the context of our current lack of knowledge about the possible role of family dynamics in the predisposition, precipitation, or perpetuation of schizophrenia.

The study suggests that the marriages of parents of schizophrenic offspring should be evaluated in a reliable and valid way for level of intimacy compared to patient and normal controls. Recent developments in the diagnosis of schizophrenia and measurement of intimacy make such a study feasible.

Moreover, a controlled trial of the effectiveness of this therapy in the management of schizophrenic patients would allow comment on the effectiveness of facilitating intimacy through cognitive self-disclosure and the influence, if any, on the course and outcome in schizophrenic illness. Finally, schizophrenic illness in offspring has been studied in relationship to parents' diagnoses, character traits, and family characteristics, but not to the experience and observation of the parents' interpersonal relationship over the life cycle. The development of reliable and valid techniques of measuring interpersonal phenomena may provide opportunities for understanding this enigmatic illness.

I have summarized a series of papers that describe the clinical development of a technique which enhances marital intimacy through facilitating cognitive self-disclosure. The remaining five chapters expand on the development of this approach since these original papers were published.

2

The Rationale

Enhancing intimacy through self-disclosure is a new approach to short-term psychotherapy for marital and family discord. It is based on several assumptions: 1) the quantity and quality of intimacy between husband and wife constitute the *single* greatest determinant of family function; 2) self-disclosure is the *single* factor which most influences a couple's level of intimacy; and 3) marital intimacy can be enhanced by facilitating *cognitive* self-disclosure.

What is intimacy? Intimate relationships are probably the most important kind of interpersonal relationships. They are felt most deeply. They provide a unique sense of attachment and belonging. Marital intimacy is not just the sum of two independently acting individuals but is a mix of two personalities which as a *dyad* has qualities not present in the actions of the isolated spouses. Erikson (1950) suggests that the development of intimacy is the major psychosocial task of young adulthood. The behavioral aspect of intimacy is predictability; the emotional aspect is a feeling of closeness; the cognitive aspect is understanding through self-disclosure; and the attitudinal aspect is commitment.

Intimacy is one of three psychological dimensions which can describe the quality of interpersonal relationships (Berman & Lief, 1975). "Boundary" and "power" are the other two psychological dimensions. *Boundary* refers to the couple's relationships in time and space to other individuals and social units. *Power* refers to the couple's capacity to resolve their conflicting needs and the style they use to resolve such differences.

Intimacy is the dimension which most determines *satisfaction* with relationships which *endure* over time. The development of intimacy is a process which depends on a variety of factors, including 1) childhood attachments; 2) the observation of and experience with one's parents' marriage; 3) one's personality; and 4) experience in personal relationships.

The quantity and quality of intimacy in a couple's relationship at a given point in time can be described by the following eight facets:

1. *Conflict resolution*—the ease with which differences of opinion are resolved.
2. *Affection*—the degree to which feelings of emotional closeness are expressed by the couple.
3. *Cohesion*—a feeling of commitment to the marriage.
4. *Sexuality*—the degree to which sexual needs are communicated and fulfilled by the marriage.
5. *Identity*—the couple's level of self-confidence and self-esteem.
6. *Compatibility*—the degree to which the couple is able to work and play together comfortably.

7. *Autonomy*—the success to which the couple gains independence from their families of origin and their offspring.
8. *Expressiveness*—the degree to which thoughts, beliefs,
   attitudes, and feelings are shared within the marriage
   (Waring et al., 1981b).

Self-disclosure is the single factor which most determines
a couple's level of intimacy (Waring & Chelune, 1983).
What is self-disclosure? Self-disclosure is the process of
verbally revealing the private self to another person and
can be classified as 1) expression of emotion; 2) expression
of need; 3) expression of thought, attitudes, beliefs, and
fantasy; and 4) self-awareness. I define the latter two as
cognitive self-disclosure.

Thus enhancing marital intimacy involves a structured
experience in which the couple disclose their beliefs, theories, and assumptions to one another in a reciprocal
pattern. The couple attempts to understand why they are
not as close as they wish to be with each other. In other
words, disclosing their assumptions about why they are
not close allows a couple a greater understanding of their
unique relationship. This process of cognitive self-disclosure enhances the couple's quantity and quality of marital
intimacy. Enhanced intimacy leads to improved family
functioning. Let us explore these assumptions in more
detail.

MARITAL INTIMACY AND FAMILY FUNCTIONING: AN INTRODUCTION

Jung (1961) emphasized that an unsatisfactory psychological relationship between the parents may be an im-

portant cause of psychogenic disorders in childhood. I believe that in all families in which one or more members experience marked anxiety or depression there is a deficiency in the quantity and/or quality of intimacy in the marriage. Satir (1967) suggested that the parents are "the architects of the family." I suggest the quality of the spouses' psychological relationship is the *foundation* on which the family is built. If the development of intimacy is the major psychosocial task of young adulthood, then it is a small step to think of intimacy as the major psychosocial task in a developing marriage and family. Couples who develop optimal intimacy build families which are adaptable and close. Couples who have optimal intimacy are generally free of anxiety and depression, and their children develop to their full potential. Failure to develop intimacy is the reason most frequently given by couples whose marriages fail.

Couples who remain together but whose intimacy is absent, deficient, or denied develop "patterns of obligatory repetition." Like individual defense mechanisms, these patterns attempt to resolve the intimacy conflict in a symbolic way, but at the same time contribute to individual stress and/or family dysfunction.

Is there evidence to support this point of view? First, let us examine the general assumptions behind this theory. I am suggesting that an interpersonal variable—the quality and quantity of intimacy—is a *necessary* but *not a sufficient* cause of an individual family member's symptoms of physical or psychological morbid anxiety or depression.

The theory suggests that any person, couple, or family who present with psychological distress will have been exposed in the past, or in the present, to a lack of intimacy. Many individuals free of symptoms will also have experienced and observed deficiencies of intimacy. Thus a deficiency in the quantity or the quality of intimacy is unlikely to be the sole cause of specific psychological distress. Lack of closeness is a contributing, initiating, or sustaining factor of more or less influence in various types of family, marital, and individual dysfunction.

Historically, Sullivan (1953) was the first to emphasize that interpersonal relationships are worth studying in attempting to understand morbid anxiety. He wrote of the development of intimacy with friends in early adolescence as an avoidance of loneliness and preparation for heterosexual relationships. Bowlby (1958) described how attachment between infant and mother is viewed as a psychological precursor of intimacy. I believe that most readers will recognize that their thinking about intimacy will have been influenced by these psychoanalysts. These concepts can be summarized as follows: 1) intimacy is thought of as an interpersonal variable; 2) the mother–child relationship is thought to be crucial to understanding intimacy; and 3) the development of intimacy is a process.

Psychologists studying personal relationships continue to debate whether there are two or three independent dimensions of these relationships (Lorr & McNair, 1963). There is general agreement that there is a power (control adaptability) dimension. Couples have to make decisions, and differences of opinion are inevitable in all relationships. Problem solving is a social skill that varies from couple to couple. One of the commonest personal problems which couples seek to resolve through outpatient psychotherapy is persistent, repetitive arguments.

The second independent dimension, which remains more controversial, is boundary (intensity, inclusion). Couples must resolve issues of independence and dependence and define the boundaries of their relationship with family, friends, and children.

The third variable is intimacy (affectivity, affection, cohesion, affiliation). Schutz (1966) found that in enduring relationships, such as marriage, closeness is the crucial variable. Lack of intimacy is the interpersonal reason most frequently offered by people seeking outpatient psychotherapy.

I have suggested that intimacy is one of three independent dimensions of personal relationships. Why select intimacy as the crucial variable for family functioning?

Kubie (1974) suggested that the core of neurosis was an "affective dysfunctional potential (−AP)." Affect is defined as the observable and measurable component of the emotional dimension of interpersonal interaction at a point in time. I have operationally defined this affective dysfunctional potential as a deficiency in the quantity and/or quality of intimacy in the marital relationship. The interpersonal relationship between husband and wife or its failure is the single enduring and constant element of any psychologically defined "family" from its inception. It is interesting to speculate why this relationship has largely been ignored as a therapeutic focus in theoretical formulations of family psychopathology.

Why select marital therapy as the focus of a theory of family dysfunction? Haley (1963) suggested that the core of the family is the "marital coalition." Family therapists have consistenly found that children with problems come from homes where there are disturbed husband–wife relationships (Ackerman, 1958; Boszormenyi-Nagy & Framo, 1965; MacGregor et al., 1964; Minuchin, 1970). In studies of normal families, Lewis et al. (1976) found that a stable parental coalition and opportunities for intimacy are important determinants of family function.

Does research support this point of view? Jacob (1975) reviewed studies of family research and found the feeling dimension to be crucial. Normal families express more positive feelings than do disturbed families. Kreitman et al.'s (1971) research on neurotic couples suggested that the variable of "affection–dislike" is independent of power, can discriminate normal from abnormal couples, is not a simple correlate of individual psychopathology, and may influence other interactional family variables. Reiss (1971) demonstrated that intimacy can influence other family variables. Quinton et al. (1976) demonstrated that marital discord predicts early behavior deviance in children.

In summary, theoretical, clinical, and research material suggest that in any interpersonal relationship that endures over time: 1) there are at least two or perhaps three independent dimensions of which an *affective variable* is one; 2) the affective dimension is powerful enough to influence other family variables and the emotional health of the offspring; and 3) the affective dimension may be the most important in enduring relationships and is consistently found to be disturbed in pathological families.

Assume for a moment that this affective variable is the quality and quantity of marital intimacy. We may ask, what are the variables that determine a couple's intimacy? How does intimacy develop? How is it best measured? Does the level of intimacy fluctuate with time, crisis, or the family life cycle? Can the level of intimacy be changed through therapy? These are the questions I address based on my clinical work and research over the past 10 years.

I begin with a review of the factors that influence the development of intimacy. This is not an exhaustive or critical review of a complex and poorly understood topic. Rather, I focus on those issues in the development of intimacy which have particular relevance to therapy. These specific issues include the quality of early attachments, the observation of and experience with one's parents' marriage, the development of one's personality, and the attraction to and selection of a spouse.

THE DEVELOPMENT OF INTIMACY IN MARRIAGE

The Quality of Early Attachments

I think most readers would agree that having a mother who was sensitive to our needs as an infant, accepting of our behavior, cooperative in our development, and accessible when approached might enhance our potential for intimacy in our marriages. While accepting that such attachments may be prototypes for adult relationships, the majority of us cannot remember our infancy. The influence of this crucial state of development remains *unconscious*. It may also be that the adult who wants to be close with his or her spouse may be motivated by factors which are independent of earlier attachments.

Jung (1971) suggests that whenever we speak of a "psychological relationship" we presuppose one that is "conscious," for there is no such thing as a psychological relationship between two people who are in a state of unconsciousness. There is in all marriages a considerable degree of partial unconsciousness, especially in the choice of the spouse. This therapy focuses almost exclusively on conscious cognition. Thus I believe the conscious observation and experience of one's parents' level of intimacy between the ages of about 4 to 10 will have a profound influence on one's capacity for intimacy. However, one must also attempt to understand the unconscious tie to the parents and conditions under which it modifies or prevents conscious choice and influences therapy. Jung suggested that children react much less to what grownups say than to the imponderables in the surrounding atmosphere. This approach focuses on the couple's conscious memories of the quality of their parents' intimacy. However, unconscious feelings, attitudes, and behavior of the couple toward the therapist may influence the course of therapy.

What we *do remember* from the age of 3 or 4 is our experience of our mother as a woman, our father as a man, both as parents, and the quality of their marriage. We grew up observing and experiencing a marriage. Paradoxically, the quality and quantity of intimacy in our parents' marriages may have influenced the degree of maternal sensitivity and acceptance we experienced as infants and children. In turn our parents may have been influenced by their own observation and experience with their parents' level of intimacy. We may also remember sharing our observations and experiences of our parents' marriages with our siblings and our friends: "Why are mom and dad always fighting?" "Why do they sleep in separate bedrooms?" "Why does father drink so much?"

Research on the quality of early attachments demonstrated that the total absence of a mother or a mother substitute during the first year of life frequently results in physical, emotional, and intellectual limitations. Where the neglect is profound, the infant can simply fail to thrive in infancy and fail to survive into adulthood. When the neglect is more emotional and no bond develops between infant and mother, many observers believe the seeds are planted for the development of the adult psychopath. This is an individual who is unable to develop intimacy with members of the opposite sex in adulthood because of an almost total absence of the capacity for empathy, understanding, or caring for another individual.

Ethologists have confirmed these observations on human infants in that severe neglect in many species, both in the laboratory and in natural surroundings, produces an adult who is incapable of mating, parenting, or peer relationships. At this extreme of total absence of mothering or severe neglect occurring in the first six months or year of life no bond develops. Erikson (1950) suggests that if the infant survives at all it survives without the capacity for basic trust—a prime factor in the development of intimacy in adulthood.

Between the ages of 1 and 3, the infant and mother develop an attachment which is based more on the quality of the mothering and the temperament of the infant. At first glance, it may appear ludicrous to consider that hereditary factors can influence an adult personality's potential for intimacy. However, the innate individual equipment of physique, temperament, and general intellectual capacity do set limits on constitutional endowment on the highly complex abilities of the adult to develop intimacy. The mother can also vary, from abuse and neglect at one extreme, to what Winnicott (1965) has termed "good enough mothering," which I already described. The quality of maternal care varies from these extremes to the more common inconsistency or overinvolvement we all may have experienced.

I refer to this stage as *attachment* because it is dependent on the quality of the relationship. Most adults can identify the qualitative tone of this period even if they cannot put it into words and remember specific instances.

Thus if any kind of mothering or caretaking occurs in the first 6 months to a year, a *bond* is formed which is intact irrespective of the quality of the mothering. But in the second stage, where an *attachment* is formed, the quality of the mothering is perceived by the infant and colors an unconscious affective tone. As examples, Bowlby (1958) describes those infants who experience "inconsistent mothering" at this time as developing anxious attachment. An infant experiencing a "neglectful or abusive mother" may experience hostile attachment and an infant experiencing an "overprotective mother" may experience a narcissistic attachment. I should like to emphasize again that these experiences are largely unconscious and may influence the kinds of unconscious expectations and attitudes which result in poorly understood behaviors in marriage. Spouses may be consistently anxious about the attachment to the spouse, continually hostile toward the spouse, or continually having expectations that the spouse will meet all of their needs, although they cannot say why!

The Observation and Experience of One's Parents' Marriage

The next major developmental stage with relevance to adult intimacy is between the ages of 3 and 5 years. The closeness which now may develop between a mother and a child is dependent on the actual qualities of their relationship and the verbal action between the two.

There are a number of psychological features at this age which may have implications for the development of adult intimacy. These include the psychological issue of separation/individuation. This involves the development in the child of a mental representation of the mother. The child maintains this mental image of mother even when the child is not in contact with her. A second important part of this phase is the development of different types of abstract thinking in the child described by Piaget (1970). A third feature is children's beginning awareness that they can choose to keep their thoughts, ideas, and feelings to themselves if they wish.

This period is culminated when the child enters school and relationships with siblings, peers, and teachers become important. It is during this time period that the child can consciously begin to remember, observe, and experience the qualitative aspects of his or her parents' relationship. Closeness at this stage is moving away from the unconscious, emotionally perceived experience depending on the affective quality of the relationship with the mother, to closeness with other figures which is dependent on self-disclosure of thoughts and feelings that the individual controls. It is at this stage that children develop best friends with whom they share secrets of their experience, thoughts, and feelings, excluding such information from their parents for the first time.

In summary, infants who do not develop a *bond* with a mother or maternal figure would appear to be incapable of developing intimacy as adults. Children who have problems in the period of *attachment* will often have profound difficulties in development of intimacy in adulthood. Children who have difficulties with *closeness* in the latency period may also have difficulties with closeness as adults.

These observations come mainly from the work of psychoanalysts, ethologists, and recent research which has directly studied the development of infants and children.

Ideally, an infant who is born to a mother who is sensitive, accepting, cooperative, and accessible will develop a strong bond to the mother. The child will develop a positive attachment and will feel close to the mother during the early phase of childhood. If the child then observes and experiences his parents having an intimate relationship with one another and has the opportunity to develop close relationships with peers, siblings, and teachers, the seeds for development of optimal intimacy have been sown. The next major developmental period is the adolescent's search for identity.

I would now like to turn to another developmental approach with implications for the process of developing identity: the development of personality. Obviously, two unique personalities interact in each marriage to produce a relationship which is more than a sum of the dyad.

The Development of Personality

How do I define personality? I use Gordon W. Allport's (1955) definition that "personality is the dynamic organization within the individual of those psychophysical systems that determine one's unique adjustment to one's environment" (p. 48).

Every personality develops continually from the stage of infancy until death. Throughout this span, one's personality persists, even though it changes. I will describe those developmental issues which determine an individual's unique adjustment to his or her marital relationships. I am describing the development of personality with particular relevance to 1) the development of identity; 2) the choice of a spouse; and 3) the development of closeness in the marital relationship.

I have already mentioned that human beings, in common with all other living creatures, are subject to the laws of heredity. Thus some important facets of personality such as physique, temperament, and mental capacity are largely determined by constitutional factors. These dimensions of personality are relatively resistant to the kind of changes I will be discussing in relationship to the enhancement of intimacy in marriage. Individuals with certain traits such as psychopathy and limited intelligence may have lower levels of intimacy. While no personality is devoid of hereditary influences, as therapists we tend, whenever possible, to stress the operation of environmental forces as they influence a developing personality's potential for intimacy in marriage.

I have already outlined the importance of key relationships in childhood which influence one's potential for intimacy. I now focus on *the mechanisms* of the developmental process rather than the relationships themselves.

The first question regards motivation. One wonders whether within the infant there is a latent propensity, instinct, or drive that will later lead him or her to seek closeness. Instinct theorists assert that there are such propensities operating prior to experience and independent of training. Thus a need for intimacy would be postulated. The evidence, however, suggests that the more sophisticated types of motives characteristic of the mature personality, such as the wish to develop a close relationship, are not found full-fledged in the newborn child.

What, then, are the basic aspects of growth and maturation that allow for these sophisticated adult sentiments? What aspects of the developmental process are available to us to understand change in therapy?

The first principle of personality development is that of *differentiation.* A psychological account of differentiation as given by Lewin suggests "the child to a greater extent than the adult is a dynamic unity. The infant acts first with its whole body and only gradually acquires the ability to execute part actions" (in Allport, 1955, p. 133). There is initially little capacity for graded response. When the 2 year old is pleased, he jumps up and down—when he is angry, he is mad all over. The infant's emotional behavior is not differentiated. When the child becomes aware of his or her autonomy at about the age of 2, the child says no to everything, much to the chagrin of most parents. This stage may be frustrating for the parent. In the next stage the child begins to ask why. This is often an even more difficult stage for the adult. Parents may be unsure of their own reasons or unprepared to reveal their reasons for demanding behaviors which have been performed automatically in the past. Also, the developing child has to this point revealed everything about himself or herself. Now the child begins to differentiate what is disclosed. Thus at about the age of 3 to 5, the stage where the relationship is based on what the parents are prepared to reveal with reference to their expectations of the child commences. The child's growing awareness that one can disclose discriminately what he is thinking develops. Cognitive self-disclosure is gradually *differentiated* from other mental functions.

The next important aspect of growth of personality is *integration.* The concept involves a gradual integration of psychological functions into a completely unified personality. The hierarchical development of such integration is believed to progress from conditioned reflexes to habits, to traits, and finally to the concept of a perfectly integrated or unique and stable personality. The importance of integration to our understanding of intimacy is that many couples come in complaining about traits of their spouse which they find unacceptable. The nature of maturation suggests that many of these traits may not be susceptible to change. This suggests that our approach might more properly address why a spouse had selected someone who had such traits which are not to their liking rather than attempt to alter integrated traits.

Another important concept in the development of personality is *learning*. Learning includes every form of acquisition and modification that occurs in the course of growth. Most psychologists when referring to learning in the sense of personality development refer to conditioning, efferent modification, and modeling.

The familiar laws of learning have some explanatory value for the development of adaptive behavior in marriage. Successful responses are retained and unsuccessful modes are lost. In close relationships we have competing principles. Practice makes perfect and so those behaviors observed and experienced in childhood will be repeated; at the other extreme those parental behaviors that were experienced as painful should be stamped out. Paradoxically what one sees is that spouses have consciously promised themselves to never behave in some of the ways their parents did in their marriage. On further examination, one finds that they are repeating patterns in spite of their best efforts. These paradoxes are an important focus for cognitive self-disclosure.

In later childhood, deliberate copying becomes an increasingly important factor in the growing personality, especially, for example, in the adoption of prejudices, beliefs, and attitudes of one's elders. Many young children learn that the assumption of a parent's attitude is a fairly safe procedure when needing a guide. Children may continue merely as uncritical inheritors of their parents' views or when childhood is past they may rebel, adopting different views. These attitudes may become a focus for exploration in cognitive family therapy.

Another fundamental issue in the development of personality with relevance to the development of intimacy is the development of *consciousness of self.*

In the young child, the development of consciousness of self is a gradual and difficult achievement. Certain reference points in the development of selfhood may be a relevant focus for therapy. For example, the infant is assigned a name at birth. The name becomes a more and more strategic point of contact between the self and the outer world. One's name is formed largely by expectations of the parents for the child of which the child is largely unaware. Exploration of these reference points may allow greater self-understanding.

In adolescence, a person attempts to define himself or herself by verbal disclosures to significant others. Their feedback as to one's accuracy of perception of self is crucial. Thus verbal disclosure of "who I am" is a critical aspect of cognitive self-disclosure.

Another developmental aspect related to intimacy is the gradual development of *self-esteem.* When a child undertakes to perform a task, one generally places one's goal at a level not so far above one's abilities that one will suffer embarrassment or humiliation. One involves oneself in tasks that one has practiced and so is less likely to fail. However, the development of heterosexual intimacy in close relationships is both novel and not practiced. Individuals may be reluctant to involve themselves in this process if they suffer from low self-esteem. These feelings of low self-esteem are important to some individuals who because of feelings of inferiority may develop conscious and unconscious strategies for compensations which avoid intimacy. Often a focus of our approach is the perception of a potential spouse as having compensatory abilities which may offset areas of deficiency which the individual perceives within himself or herself.

Another issue in the process of developing an adult personality is the formation of the *unconscious mental mechanisms of defense.* In marital relationships, several mental mechanisms including rationalization, projection, and self-justification may cause discord. Reason fits one's impulses and beliefs to the world of reality. Rationalization and self-justification fit one's conception of reality to one's impulses and beliefs. Reasoning discovers true reasons and rationalization and self-justification good reasons. These unconscious mental mechanisms often are elements of relationships that are not close. Quite a different example of rationalization is that form known as projection. It may be defined as a type of self-deception by which a person ascribes his own secret thoughts, wishes, and shortcomings to another person. All of these relate to attempts by individuals to maintain their self-esteem through their marital relationships, and are related to the difficulty in self-disclosure which people with low self-esteem experience.

Allport (1955) suggested that in order to understand the dynamics of the normal, mature personality, a new and somewhat radical principle of growth must be introduced to supplement the more traditional developmental concepts thus far considered. For convenience of discussion this new principle may be called the *functional autonomy* of motives. The dynamic psychology proposed here regards adult motives for intimacy as infinitely varied and self-sustaining. Contemporary relationships may grow out of antecedent relationships but may also be functionally independent of them.

Finally, optimal intimacy in our developmental discussion of personality is more likely to occur in a relationship between two fully mature personalities. Again, Allport has described the mature personality as having three features. The first is a variety of autonomous interests. This means that the individual can lose himself in work, in contemplation, in recreation, and in loyalty to others. In the mature personality, the goals and attitudes represent an extension of the self.

The second factor is called self-objectification, that peculiar detachment of mature persons when they survey their own pretensions and abilities. Coupled with this, Allport suggested that maturity involves the capacity for insight and a sense of humor. Cognitive self-disclosure may help develop the individual's self-objectification.

The third factor in the mature personality is the unifying philosophy of life. Such a philosophy is not necessarily articulated but influences his or her expectations of interpersonal relationships. Again, self-disclosure involves an articulation of this unifying philosophy of life.

Thus different types of mature personalities bring different expectations with them to their marital relationship. For example, the dominant interest of the theoretical person is the discovery of truth. In this interpersonal relationship, honest closeness will be a major priority. The economical person is characterized by usefulness and so the marriage will be expected to be practically important. The highest value for the social type of personality is love of people, whether conjugal or filial, and closeness itself may be an important goal. The political person is primarily interested in power. Mature personalities may have some awareness of which of these dominant motifs is theirs. Conflict is produced when spouses have inaccurate perceptions of themselves.

Recently, we identified some traits of personality which are associated with optimal intimacy. These traits suggest that spouses who are by nature cautious, reliable, and curious about what their spouses are thinking have close relationships. On the other hand, people with traits of neuroticism and introversion have difficulty in maintaining close relationships.

In summary, the processes described in the development of personality have implications for the quality of interpersonal relationships. One cannot help but be impressed by how often the issue of self-disclosure becomes critical as an element of personality development as it relates to intimacy.

Now I turn to a final developmental perspective which may help in our understanding of the process of developing intimacy in close relationships. This is the approach of social psychology which describes how distant relationships become close ones. This approach addresses the question of how close relationships develop from the initial superficial encounter to marital relationships.

The Attraction to and Selection of a Spouse

Social psychologists studying interpersonal relationships are interested in the factors that influence interpersonal attraction: why we like or are liked by others and how relationships develop into friendship, love, and marriage. One model which traces the development of interpersonal relationship from attraction to love has been developed by Levinger and Snoek (1972). This model hypothesizes that people go through a series of stages or levels as relationships develop. These levels are termed zero contact, awareness, surface contact, and mutuality. At each level, different factors are important as determinants of attraction.

Obviously, considering all of the people who are around us in relation to the number of people actually known, most people coexist at the zero-contact level. Even though two people have no relationship, it is important to know what factors will lead to their becoming aware of one another and thus beginning a relationship. The most important determinant of such awareness is called *propinquity,* meaning physical closeness. In spite of the fact that most of us feel that we have free will in choosing relationships and partners, it is surprising how often potential spouses live in close physical proximity. It may be that you have attended the same high school, worked in the same place, attended the same social or recreational functions, or attended the same university. Thus the physical proximity also implies a certain compatibility of social class, values, and experiences.

The next stage of relationship development is the level of awareness in which one person is aware of the other, the "familiar stranger." There is no actual interaction at this point in time. One's impression of the other is based on observable external characteristics such as physical attractiveness, clothing, the way a person seems to act or reputational factors conveyed by people who know the individual. While social psychologists have suggested that this stage of awareness is heavily influenced by *physical attractiveness,* psychoanalysts have suggested that this physical attractiveness is also determined by *unconscious factors.* It is in fact remarkable that when couples with difficulty are asked why they were initially attracted to one another, they frequently say they weren't! Many say they were physically attracted but cannot identify why or simply state that they like one another, but have little understanding of this. This important awareness stage thus becomes a focus for greater understanding in cognitive self-disclosure. It is also surprising how couples instinctively select someone who has had a similar family background whether painful or pain-free (Skynner & Cleese, 1983).

The next level is surface contact and the nature of this interaction is superficial and predictable. The individuals will probably ask each other questions regarding such things as studies, interests, hobbies, and attitudes. The couple will engage in typical courtship and dating behavior. The important principle in this stage is the issue of *conscious reinforcement.* That is, liking occurs when two people find that interacting with one another is reinforcing. It should be noted that reinforcement in this stage cannot be one-sided. Social exchange theory emphasizes that for the relationship to continue each person must reinforce the other.

A second important aspect of this stage of relationship development is *attitude similarity.* Through the process of mutual self-disclosure one begins to reveal more deep-seated facets of the personality including attitudes, beliefs, and values. Once again, as before, attitude similarity leads to liking and to increased feelings of closeness. One of the difficulties for courtship in North America in this particular stage is the issue of social approval. Young people are often trained to present socially desirable facets of their personality or to present a persona which they believe is what their partner is looking for in the relationship. As a result of this lack of self-disclosure, couples frequently are surprised to find after they have become engaged and married that they may have radically different attitudes or values with reference to religion, child-rearing, or sexuality.

The final level of this developmental theory is described as *mutuality* and is a continuum in which the two people's lives begin to overlap more and more. Thus the couple begins to address issues of their boundary by the socially acceptable stages of going steady, engagement, and finally marriage with its implication for who is included and who is excluded from the couple's relationship. The couple also begins to spend more and more time together. They begin to interact in ways that lead to further self-disclosure and also give indications of their capacity to meet sex role–specific aspects of marital relationships.

Social psychologists have also discussed the development of mutuality: whether need compatibility or need complementarity is most important for the development of closeness in relationships. Put colloquially, do "opposites attract" or do "birds of a feather flock together"? Need complementarity occurs when the two have needs that are opposite and complementary. For example, the person who is high on a need to give love will select a person who is high on a need to receive love. Evidence suggests that during initial stages of close relationships such complementary situations work well *but* over the long term of marital relationships they lead to frustrations and difficulties. Distressed couples will often present problems related to a spouse saying that he or she married for security and stability, but now find it stifling and boring. Therapy then must address the issue of why the individual lacked this stability and security and why he or she believed that someone else could provide it.

Murstein (1974) developed his *stimulus-value-role theory* suggesting that in a relatively free-choice situation, attraction and interaction depend on the value of the assets and liabilities each of the individuals brings to the relationship. The kinds of variables that influence the course of development of the relationship can be classified under three categories: stimulus, value comparison, and role. Murstein suggests that potential spouses meet in an environment in which stimulus variables are most important during the beginning of the relationship. Surface factors such as physical attractiveness, voice and speech patterns, coordination, mode of dress, and reputational factors are more influential when they are encountered in an open field.

In the second stage, if the couple has fairly equal values with reference to interests, attitudes, beliefs, and sometimes needs, they are revealed through the process of self-disclosure. The stimulus stage can perhaps be thought of as an awareness period, the value stage as attitudes revealed by self-disclosure, and the role stage as a behavioral period.

With couples with relationship difficulties, it is consistently found that the value comparison stage was never satisfactorily explored and self-disclosure was absent. Murstein suggests that the role stage is a crucial one, for it is here that the couple can compare the ways they actually behave toward one another in comparison to the way that they would like to behave to one another. One sees couples who present with difficulties, who, if they have gone through this stage, have chosen to ignore difficulties in role development in day-to-day interaction. They seem to believe that these issues will be resolved after the marriage. So we can see that the actual behavior, the "bottom line" of the relationship, is most influential in the role stage. Its implications for therapy would be to explore why the difficulties in this stage were ignored. Finally, Lewis (1972) developed a theory of premarital dyadic formation, rather than a theory of actual mate selection, although the two are closely linked. He proposes a six-stage process: 1) the achievement by pairs of perceived similarity; 2) the achievement of pair rapport; 3) the achievement of openness between partners through mutual self-disclosure; 4) the achievement of role-taking accuracy; 5) the achievement of personal role fit; and 6) the achievement of dyadic crystallization.

In summary, I have briefly reviewed three perspectives on the development of interpersonal relationships, particularly as they pertain to the development of intimacy in marriage. Each developmental approach has implications for a therapy designed to assist couples with difficulty in their close marital relationships. However, each approach has some deficiencies in and of itself.

The psychoanalysts and ethologists stress the importance of earlier relationships on later relationship development but ignore the principle of functional autonomy which suggests that adult motives for intimacy may be distinct and different from childhood motives for closeness. The personality theorists suggest important mechanisms of learning which may be explored in therapy but largely ignore the issue that even two mature personalities may have a difficult interpersonal interaction, which is not explained solely by the development of the personalities themselves. Finally, the social psychologists provide descriptions of how relationships develop but ignore entirely the influence of the personality, earlier relationships, and unconscious factors.

However, taking the three developmental approaches together, one is impressed by how each approach emphasizes the fundamental importance of *self-disclosure* in the development of *intimacy*. The three developmental theories also suggest aspects of the development of intimacy which may be explored to provide relevant content for understanding closeness through self-disclosure. These aspects include the observation and experience of individuals of their parents' level of intimacy during their developmental years; their development of their own identities; the reasons—both conscious and unconscious—for attraction and spouse selection; the period of self-disclosure during courtship; and the relative acceptance or rejection of various traits of the partner during marital interaction. This section has not been an exhaustive or critical review but an overview to introduce the reader to both the complexity of the topic and the common themes that are explored further in the chapters on assessment and therapy.

THE MEASUREMENT OF MARITAL INTIMACY

I think that the quality and quantity of intimacy in a marriage constitute the single most important factor in marital satisfaction and family function. Optimal intimacy is associated with the absence of anxiety and depression in both spouses. Optimal intimacy produces a family environment characterized by adaptiveness and cohesion. This operational definition of intimacy was developed in the context of a theory which attempts to explain why some families have members with emotional disorders and other families do not. If this operational definition of marital intimacy can be measured with reliability and validity, a test of the hypothesis is possible.

Initially, several studies were done to evaluate what facets of marital intimacy needed to be measured. The first study involved asking couples in the general population what intimacy meant to them (Waring et al., 1980). The second study involved the completion of several self-report questionnaires regarding facets of marriage to evaluate which elements were associated with marital adjustment (Waring et al., 1981b). A third study involved interviewing and videotaping couples with marital discord and nonpsychotic emotional illness and comparing them to couples who were adjusted. Differences that might help us identify intimacy were identified (Waring et al., 1984). These studies were completed in the absence of a specific review of other researchers' operational definitions of intimacy, although these were eventually explored. These operational definitions are available to the interested reader in a review by Schaefer and Olson (1981). We developed a standardized, structured interview as well as a self-report questionnaire based on the eight facets of intimacy which have been mentioned previously and are defined as follows:

1. *Conflict resolution*—the ease with which differences of opinion are resolved.
2. *Affection*—the degree to which feelings of emotional closeness are expressed by the couple.
3. *Cohesion*—a feeling of commitment to the marriage.
4. *Sexuality*—the degree to which sexual needs are communicated and fulfilled by the marriage.

5. *Identity*—the couple's level of self-confidence and self-esteem.
6. *Compatibility*—the degree to which the couple is able to work and play together comfortably.
7. *Autonomy*—the success with which the couple gains independence from their families of origin and their offspring.
8. *Expressiveness*—the degree to which thoughts, beliefs, attitudes, and feelings are shared within the marriage.

The structured interview, the Victoria Hospital Intimacy Interview (VHII), included ratings on "overall intimacy" and "intimate behavior" observed during the interview. The self-report questionnaire contains a control scale for social desirability. The interview and the questionnaire both have acceptable reliability and validity, which is reported elsewhere (Waring, 1984; Waring et al., 1981a; Waring & Reddon, 1983).

Why are the operational definition and the measurement instruments important to the development of this approach? I think readers are able to evaluate whether my definition of intimacy corresponds to their own ideas about intimacy. The operational definition allows you to evaluate whether some facet included or some facet excluded might improve the operational definition.

But perhaps of more importance, the operational definition can be used to explain intimacy to couples, develop therapy contracts with couples, and identify strengths and weaknesses in couples. First, when explaining cognitive self-disclosure to couples, I suggest the therapy is designed to enhance marital intimacy. The couple is able to judge experientially whether they think they are not as close as they wish to be, and they can objectively compare their level of intimacy to that of other couples. The couple is also able to identify which facets of intimacy in their relationship need greater understanding and which facets are satisfactory. For example, couples in which one or both spouses have psychosomatic symptoms often have a pattern of high commitment, positive identity, high compatibility, and good conflict resolution combined with deficiencies in sexuality, expression of affection, autonomy, and self-disclosure. This knowledge allows couples who feel their marriage is adjusted to recognize specific areas of strength, which increases rapport while focusing on the particular deficiencies. Finally, the objective measures of intimacy allow for couples to assess their progress, therapists to recognize therapeutic impasses, and for outcome studies on the effectiveness, efficiency, and humane qualities of this approach.

These objective measures have also allowed us to develop operational definitions of four types of marital intimacy and their prevalence both in the general population and in specific patient groups (Waring et al., 1986). These four types of intimacy are discussed next.

Optimal Intimacy

One in every ten couples who marry will develop optimal intimacy. The spouses come from families characterized by open communication and intimacy. They have had close relationships with parents, siblings, and peers. They know who they are, what they want to do, and who they want to be within relationships.

Such couples are enjoyable to interview and share a sense of humor. Their values, goals, and attitudes are so similar that they rarely have differences of opinion. They verbally express respect, caring, loving, and liking. They are committed to their marriage, which is their most important relationship. The couple is actively involved with extended family, friends, and community. They communicate in an open, honest, and respectful manner and disclose their private thoughts to each other.

Optimally intimate families rarely visit physicians except for serious accidents or illness. Sociologists find such couples dull, traditional, and stereotyped. The media find them boring. Mental health professionals are cynical about their happiness. These responses notwithstanding, the optimally intimate couples show remarkable physical and emotional health and stable family environments.

Adequate Intimacy

Two of every ten couples develop adequate marital intimacy. Adequate intimacy is neither a statistical nor a cultural norm. Essentially, this type of intimacy involves areas of strength and areas of weakness in the relationship, but weaknesses such as lack of compatibility or difficulties with sexuality are perceived accurately and acknowledged by both, and the strengths outweigh the weaknesses. These couples may attend marital enrichment programs or seek marital counseling for specific problems. Typically, a couple who is very committed, compatible, and caring may have a specific sexual problem or recurrent argument which they do not understand, and they seek professional help. Because of other strengths, these couples do extremely well with professional help, but the majority simply accept and adjust to their difficulties.

Pseudo-Intimacy

These couples have more areas of weakness than strength in their intimate relationships, but for a variety of reasons they attempt to make a good impression. Two out of every ten couples who marry develop a pattern of pseudo-intimacy. Although the spouses hunger for intimate love relationships, they settle for the symbols of marital adjustment and the sense of a family. The most commonly seen pattern of pseudo-intimacy is where one spouse, usually the wife, perceives the relationship as lacking in affection and compatibility and feels she does not have a close, confiding relationship with her husband. The husband, however, does not perceive or acknowledge these difficulties. The wife may stay in the relationship for the benefit of the children, for social acceptability, or because of fears or insecurities, but she will seek medical help for symptoms of anxiety or depression.

A second example is a patient with chronic pain who says her marriage is fine, her husband supportive, and they never argue. On close evaluation, one often finds they never argue because they never express themselves; the husband is solicitous, but there is no genuine affection and no sexuality and the couple maintains the facade of marital adjustment through social isolation.

A final example is the pseudo-mutuality of families where the marriage is characterized by pseudo-intimacy. A couple who refuse or who are unable to perceive their lack of intimacy may focus criticism, attention, or expressed emotion on a child, who may become a scapegoat to maintain the fragile stability of a family.

Deficient or Absent Intimacy

Two out of every ten couples who marry stay together despite lack of overt closeness between the spouses. In-

terestingly, the statistical average for marriage in our society, the median couple, is between pseudo-intimacy and
deficient intimacy, a far cry from our cultural myths about
marriage.

Marriages with deficient intimacy are characterized by
open discord, physical abuse, alcoholism, affairs, chronic
grudges, alliances with children, and chaotic family life.
Although they lack affection, have poor communication,
frequent arguments, and poor sexuality, these couples are
surprisingly committed and there are moments of joy in
the chaotic family life. Physicians become involved with
these couples through suicide attempts, alcoholism, venereal disease, and antisocial behavior on the part of the
children.

Divorce

Three out of every ten couples who marry will separate
and/or divorce. Some couples will never develop any
closeness and some will lose an attachment irrespective of
their level of intimacy. The couples who recognize they
have not made a genuine commitment, such as those who
married because of a premarital pregnancy or who battle
for control, may not develop intimacy. These separations
or divorces may allow both an opportunity for counseling
to carefully explore their reasons for marital choice.

Couples who have developed some degree of intimacy
present a different problem. There is evidence that the
time between the breaking of affectionate ties in the relationship and actual physical separation or divorce is the
period of greatest vulnerability for depression and suicide
attempts. This period can last longer than two years for
many of these couples.

RESEARCH ON MARITAL INTIMACY, NEUROSIS, AND FAMILY FUNCTIONING

My theory of family discord suggests that deficiencies in the quality and/or quantity of marital intimacy will be associated with symptoms of nonpsychotic emotional illness in one or both spouses and deficiencies in family functioning. The absence of an intimate, confiding relationship has been identified as a vulnerability factor in the onset of depression under adverse circumstances (Brown & Harris, 1978). Aneschenel and Stone (1982) suggest that, assuming that lack of perceived social support is not just a manifestation of depression itself, lack of intimacy may contribute to the creation of depressive symptoms independent of life events. Birtchnell and Kennard (1983) present data suggesting poor marital quality is associated with neurotic depression. Tennant, Hurry, and Bebbington (1982) suggest that adult depression may be related to childhood separations between the ages of 5 and 10 where some of the separations were related to the quality of the marriage. Fredin (1982) suggests that depressed individuals have inadequate depth contact with their partners. Mitchell et al. (1983) suggest the level of support available from one's spouse is an important factor in the development of depressive symptoms. Waring and Patton (1984a) demonstrated a significant association between the severity of depression and deficiencies of marital intimacy. Those hospitalized depressed patients with the lowest levels of marital intimacy failed to improve at follow-up. Waring, Reddon, et al. (1983), in a study of 69 nonclinical couples, found support for the empirical relationships between deficiencies of marital intimacy and abnormal mood states.

Henderson et al. (1980) suggest that the perceived availability and adequacy with which significant others meet an individual's requirements for attachment play a small but significant role in the onset of nonpsychotic emotional illness under adverse circumstances. Waring et al. (1981b) found that deficiencies of marital intimacy were significantly associated with the presence of symptoms of non-psychotic emotional illness in one or both spouses. Patton and Waring (1984), in a sample of patients with nonpsy-chotic emotional illness, found that marital intimacy was significantly lower in all eight facets of intimacy in comparison to a nonpatient sample. In a study of 250 couples in the general population, nonpsychotic emotional illness was found to be particularly associated with average and absent intimacy (Waring et al., 1986).

It is well known that correlation is a necessary but not a sufficient condition for inferring cause. These studies all simply employ correlational analysis and cannot lead to the inference that deficiences of marital intimacy cause depression and neurosis. However, the results of all of these studies are generally consistent with the expectations based on the theory of family psychopathology. The theory has been given empirical support by showing that these relationships exist across diverse samples, both clinical and nonclinical, and with widely varying techniques of measuring marital intimacy and neurosis. The possibility also exists that nonpsychotic emotional illness may prevent the development of intimacy or a common factor such as neurotic character traits or lack of self-disclosure may influence both. In summary, since a significant empirical correlation does exist between "optimal" levels of intimacy and the absence of help-seeking behavior for neurotic symptoms, the assumption that enhancing marital intimacy may relieve symptoms of neurosis seems plausible.

Finally, Lewis et al. (1976) suggest that opportunities for intimacy are an important element of normal family functioning. The development of intimacy is considered the major psychosocial task of young adulthood. Since marriages initiate the family life cycle, one might expect family functioning and the family environment to be determined to a significant degree by the quality and quantity of marital intimacy. Obviously, a variety of other factors also influence family functioning and environment. Clearly, couples do not marry and have families only in order to develop closeness, but intimacy is a psychological variable which may offer an opportunity for therapeutic change. If one could demonstrate a relationship between measures of marital intimacy and family function or environment, this would provide further support for our theory.

Recently, measures of family environment and family function have become available (Moos & Moos, 1976; Olson, Russell, & Sprenkle, 1979). In a pilot study of patients with nonpsychotic emotional illness, deficiencies of marital intimacy were significantly associated with abnormal family environment and with patterns of chaos and enmeshment (Waring & Patton, 1984b). While this preliminary study supports the theory of family psychopathology, it must be viewed with some caution, as 1) the sample was not a general population sample; 2) only the married couples participated and not their children; 3) the self-report questionnaires were the only assessment instruments used; and 4) results represent only correlations. However, the opportunity for prospective studies on families utilizing a variety of reliable and valid measurements of intimacy and family functioning are now clearly feasible.

INTIMACY AND SELF-DISCLOSURE

Self-disclosure, the revelation of personal information to another, has been implicated as an important factor in the development of interpersonal intimacy. Jourard (1971) argued that authentic self-disclosure is an important means for decreasing interpersonal distance and a prerequisite for developing intimate relationships. Some have argued that self-disclosure and intimacy are synonymous (Cozby, 1973). If this is true, then the previous discussion of intimacy is superfluous. It is possible that the relationship between deficiencies of intimacy and the presence of neurosis is explained by a fundamental problem with self-disclosure which explains both phenomena.

Others have suggested a curvilinear relationship between intimacy and self-disclosure. This hypothesis suggests a certain amount of self-disclosure produces closeness, but too much will produce distance. Waterman (1980) reviewed several studies that had found a positive relationship between self-report measures of self-disclosure and expressed marital satisfaction. Our operational definition of intimacy does not have a separate category for self-disclosure. Our assumption has been that the process of self-disclosure is an important determinant of level of intimacy, but it is not identical. I assume that the amount of self-disclosure can be therapeutically altered with a positive effect on level of intimacy. I next briefly review some research that lends support to these assumptions.

Gordon Chelune and I (Waring & Chelune, 1983) collaborated on a study in which videotapes of couples being interviewed about the quality of their marriages were rated independently by raters trained to measure aspects of self-disclosure. There were 10 couples without relationship or personal difficulties and 10 couples with problems. Each couple's level of intimacy was rated independently. The amount of self-disclosure, congruence, positive or negative self-reference, and level of personal revelation were measured.

The major finding was that a combined score of the various facets of self-disclosure explained about half of the variance in the intimacy ratings. Self-disclosing behavior is a major determinant of how close a couple seems to an observer. Furthermore, the relationship was a linear one, which meant the greater the self-disclosure the higher the intimacy. The couple's identity, compatibility, expressiveness, and intimate behavior were the facets of intimacy most influenced by self-disclosure. In summary, although self-disclosure and intimacy are *not* the same, the greater the self-disclosure the higher the ratings of intimacy.

Finally, the ratings of self-disclosure could differentiate the problem couples from the normal couples. The aspects of self-disclosure which most clearly differentiated the couples were positive self-reference and congruent disclosures found in the normal couples. In summary, if one could train couples to increase the number of positive or neutral self-references and encourage disclosure in a manner where affect (feeling) and content (thought) were congruent, one might enhance their level of intimacy.

ENHANCING MARITAL INTIMACY THROUGH FACILITATING COGNITIVE SELF-DISCLOSURE

I have suggested that some deficiencies in the quality and/or quantity of marital intimacy are associated with anxiety, depression, and psychosomatic symptoms as well as disturbances in the family environment. Any technique which enhances intimacy should relieve symptoms and improve family functioning. Thus improving sexual functioning, assisting problem solving, increasing expression of affection, improving communication, elevating self-esteem, ensuring compatibility, expanding social network, and enhancing commitment would all be expected to improve marital satisfaction. In fact all of these suggestions are the basis of various forms of counseling that do have positive effects on individual emotional health, marital satisfaction, and family functioning. Some of these goals appear easier to accomplish than others, but all will enhance intimacy.

I have suggested that since self-disclosure has such a profound influence on intimacy, facilitating self-disclosure may be both the easiest and the most direct technique for enhancing intimacy. In fact, there is considerable evidence to suggest that if one increases the amount of self-disclosure between spouses, if the disclosures are positive and congruent, if the content is perceived as relevant by both spouses, and if both spouses are perceived as listening, the level of intimacy will be enhanced.

Why cognitive self-disclosure? First, couples with problems often wish to disclose their feelings. These feelings are rarely positive. One could ask them to express affection, liking, loving, or kindness, but they might refuse or the expression might not be congruent. They want to express their anger, hurt, and criticism, but we know this will produce distance. Even when they express this negative affect, our next question is a cognitive exploration of why they experience these emotions. So the focus on cognitive self-disclosure produces an active suppression of the negative feelings which lead to distance.

What is the information that will be perceived as relevant? I start with each spouse's theory about why the couple has not been able to develop the closeness they wish. Initially, the spouses often have very different theories. We explore the origin of these ideas and the attitudes, beliefs, and values that influence their thinking. Frequently

their observations of their parents' relationship will enhance this proccess of self-disclosure.

Thus each spouse is allowed an opportunity to answer
the therapist's cognitive questions about his or her motivations, perceptions, and theories while the other spouse
listens. When one spouse is unable to go further, the
therapist turns to the other spouse and says, "What were
you thinking while your spouse was talking?" This alternating pattern of self-disclosure, usually lasting three to
five minutes, facilitates cognitive self-disclosure in a reciprocal pattern.

This relatively simple *technique* is the essence of Cognitive Family Therapy. The therapist's questions become
more sophisticated with experience. The disclosures become
more personal and revealing. Consistent patterns of disclosure emerge. The spouses soon begin to assist their
mates when unable to continue. The couple reveal previously undisclosed attitudes or motivations for marriage.
They see similar patterns to those observed in their parents.
They begin to speculate about their parents' motives. The
therapist may disclose ideas or theories which are suggested
by the material.

But the process remains the same. The therapist continues to facilitate the couple's cognitive self-disclosure to
each other to enhance their intimacy. The following chapters describe the process of therapy. I think the reader
may be ready to leave the theory behind and experience
the process of cognitive self-disclosure!

"What were you thinking while you read this chapter?"

3

Assessment

This chapter follows the course of an assessment interview designed to evaluate marital intimacy from referral to the development of a treatment contract. Only the spouses are considered in most of the chapter, although I briefly describe how the assessment is done with the children present. The format is relatively structured and I will explain the reasons for the development of this interview format.

REFERRAL

An assessment interview with a couple is a unique experience. Couples seldom reveal the private side of their relationship spontaneously to an outsider. Unique experiences have the potential for good or bad outcomes. Couples who have a bad experience in an initial assessment will seldom return for therapy. I attempt to make every initial assessment a positive experience.

All referrals are initiated by one spouse or the other. Only one spouse can be on the telephone to arrange the details of an initial appointment. One spouse may be interviewed when the suggestion of a conjoint assessment is made. Often one spouse will initiate referral with the other spouse absent. The absent spouse is obviously at a disadvantage at the initial assessment.

When one spouse calls to make an appointment, I usually insist on a conjoint interview and decline to listen to the presenting complaint. Often my secretary will handle the referral. I explain that I prefer to start with both spouses present so that neither spouse will feel a disadvantage and because I am not a good telephone listener (which is true). If the spouse insists on an individual assessment, I agree only if that person agrees that everything which is discussed can be revealed to the other spouse. This usually terminates the request for the private interview. My experience has been that these requests are often made to reveal secrets, which will make any efforts to assist the couple fruitless. Often these requests are made to ensure the therapist will be an advocate for the one spouse's point of view. Occasionally the referral process ends at this point.

Frequently I interview spouses who are referred for symptoms of psychiatric distress such as depression or the physical or psychological symptoms of anxiety. If the patient attributes these symptoms to his or her marriage or spends most of the time talking about marital distress, I will suggest a conjoint interview. Obviously many patients will refuse this assessment, wishing to pursue therapy on an individual basis.

More often patients respond that their spouses will not be willing to attend. I ask for their theories of why they think the spouse will refuse. I also ask them to demonstrate how they would invite the spouse. This frequently reveals why refusal might occur.

"Dr. Waring wants to talk to you about your alcoholism." "I told the psychiatrist about your temper and he thinks you have a problem." "I set up an interview to talk about our rotten sex life." Perhaps it is not so surprising that these spouses might not show up. Many spouses want you to hear only their side of the story. They are often not looking for change in the relationship so much as ventilation and self-justification. Many people derive peace of mind from a common rationalization: were it not for their spouses, they would be the happiest people on earth.

I rehearse with patients how to invite the spouse to an assessment interview. "I hope you will join me to discuss our arguments, which I don't understand, but know I contribute to starting." Statements that identify relationship problems which are shared and an interview which is only an assessment are more likely to be successful. I offer to speak to the spouse if there are concerns or questions. In spite of these efforts, some spouses will not come, but I leave the door open and occasionally months or years later an initial assessment takes place.

Referral sources often provide no specific information about a couple. Frequently the referral source has no detailed information about marital distress. If couples have had previous therapy, I am always interested in the perceived reasons why this was unsuccessful as the same problem often recurs quickly with new therapists. Often the referral source is aware of the more overtly disturbing behavior or suffering of one or the other spouse.

Assessment interviews commence when the couple and I are comfortably together in my office. I do a fair number of assessments in a one-way viewing room for teaching purposes. Couples are always informed well in advance of such arrangements. Frequently a student sits in on these interviews and actively participates.

INTERVIEWING SKILLS

I discuss briefly only those skills which have particular relevance to the specific marital intimacy assessment interview. These include 1) structuring the interview and providing information; 2) activity level of the interviewer; 3) control of the interview; and 4) the suppression of negative feelings.

Couples do not know what to expect when they arrive for an initial assessment interview. They are frequently and understandably apprehensive. I explain to them in some detail that the interview is an assessment *only* and that no commitment for treatment has been made by the couple or me. I explain that if there are subjects that one or both do not wish to discuss I will respect their wishes. I describe to them the areas of their relationship that will be covered during the interview. Obviously this involves a lot of talking on my part during the initial stages of the interview. I also disclose the specific areas of interpersonal relationships which I think are important. I ask them how they *feel* about the assessment and allow time to explore the cognitive reasons why one or both may be reluctant to be in the interview. I also ask whose idea the assessment was and why the other spouse agreed.

I think you will have deduced that the interviewer is very active during the assessment. There are several important reasons for this activity. First, the activity is reassuring to most couples involved in a unique experience. Second, passivity in an assessment interview often results in the couple demonstrating the relationship problems such as arguments in the presence of the interviewer. While the observation of a couple's interaction may be a focus of intervention for certain therapists, in an initial interview before a contract is made, the couple may despair that a problem they cannot control or understand is also not controlled or understood by the interviewer. Third, the therapist's activity prevents the defensive use of emotional reaction to avoid listening. Finally, it allows for a balanced interview where both spouses equally disclose their cognitions, and both positive as well as negative issues in the past and present are completely covered. Passivity on the part of the interviewer often results in the couple focusing on the current unresolved dilemma without understanding or resolution.

The activity of the interviewer is a component of the control that should be maintained. Control of the interview involves avoidance of couple behaviors that produce negative outcomes in unique experiences. Spouses must be prevented from using the interview for self-exposure which involves ultimatums, personal attacks, domination, and attempts to advocate that the interviewer make value judgments, take sides, or give advice about separation or divorce. The interviewer must control the pace of the assessment as well as his own tendency to emotional reaction.

Finally, every effort should be made to control the expression of negative feeling. Couples arrive with criticisms, bitterness, frustrations, grudges, and despair. Evidence suggests strongly that expression of negative feelings leads to distance between spouses. The couple have usually

expressed negative feelings prior to assessment and repetition will lead to hopelessness and despair.

THE INTERVIEW

The interview begins with introductions and attempts
to develop rapport through ventilation about the couple's
feelings about the assessment as well as neutral demo-
graphic questions: years of marriage, number of children,
living arrangements, and source of referral. Sometimes
these questions are not so neutral!

PRESENTING PROBLEM

Both spouses are given the opportunity to disclose their
perceptions of the presenting problem and I am able to
evaluate whether there is agreement. The most commonly
cited interpersonal problems are persistent arguments, drifting apart, poor communication, or a recent affair, separation, or mutually distressing incident. Frequently the
presenting problem is some trait or behavior of the other
spouse which is distressing. Less frequent is the complaint
that a spouse is eliciting symptoms of psychiatric illness
such as alcoholism or depression.

This is the point at which the marital intimacy assessment
interview departs from other evaluation models. Very little
time is spent on the presenting problem because the couple
have been unable to resolve or understand the problem.
The couple often express anger in their descriptions of the
presenting problem. This segment lasts only about five
minutes.

The couple are next asked what their theories are about why the presenting problem exists. They are asked why arguments occur in their relationship. If they have no specific ideas about themselves, they may be asked why arguments occur in other relationships they know about or in couples in general. They may be asked their theories of why the other spouse is "selfish" or "controlling" and why they selected such a person to marry. The questions begin the process of cognitive self-disclosure. The spouses' theories often are discrepant. This segment of the interview usually takes 5 to 10 minutes depending on the psychological mindedness and interpersonal curiosity of the couple.

ATTRACTION, DATING, COURTSHIP

The couple are next asked about how they met and why they were attracted to each other (although couples with marital distress sometimes were not attracted initially). For most couples this involves some happy memories and occasional humor. These questions also take the couple away from the anger and frustration of the presenting problem. The information is always interesting, ranging from blind dates, chance meetings, high school romances, to arranged marriages. Distressed couples often are unable to verbalize the attributes which attracted them to their future spouse. The couple are asked about their families' reactions to their spouses. Questions about courtship, engagement, and the wedding follow. This segment usually takes 10 to 15 minutes and continues the process of cognitive self-disclosure.

PARENTS' LEVEL OF INTIMACY

Next the couple are asked about their observations and experiences with their parents' marriages. This is often the first time the spouses have been asked to put their perceptions of the quality of their parents' relationships into words. Spouses will describe persistent arguments, lack of affection or sleeping in separate bedrooms, divorce or separation, alcoholism, and a variety of specific problems. A consistent observation is that the behavior of one parent is often blamed for the parents' marital problems, and there is an inability to think about what the other parent did to contribute to the problems. Occasionally a spouse will say that his or her parents "seemed" to have a good marriage and emphasize that the parents are still together. The other spouse will often contribute an observation of difficulties he or she has observed. Both spouses are asked their thoughts about how these examples of marital discord affected them personally. The common response is that they consciously made themselves a promise not to repeat the problems or they wished to avoid marrying a person like the parent they perceived as contributing most to the discord. Most couples report that this is the first time they have disclosed some of this information to their spouse and the process allows an assessment of each spouse's interpersonal curiosity. This segment lasts about 10 minutes.

FAMILY LIFE CYCLE

A chronological history of the marriage is now taken starting from the honeymoon, which often allows a neutral introduction to any specific sexual problems. The birth of children and the couple's ideas about how this influenced their relationship are explored. This allows the couple to identify the point at which each perceived dissatisfaction with the marriage developing and why they believed the discord was developing. Couples will identify problems with establishing boundaries for the relationship in the early years relating to premarital pregnancies, overinvolvement with family of origin, or unwillingness to give up previous life style. Problems from three to five years usually revolve around issues of power such as career decisions, living arrangements, or child care. Issues of intimacy from five to seven years are surprisingly commonly referred to as the "seven-year itch." Parenting problems are often encountered during the next 10 to 20 years, followed by issues of boredom or the empty nest. Specific issues of illness, unemployment, remarriage, and emotional illness may be revealed. This segment lasts about 10 minutes.

CURRENT RELATIONSHIP

In this final 10-minute segment, we bring the couple back to the present by evaluating the eight facets of intimacy in their current relationship. How do you as a couple express affection? How committed are you to this relationship? How do you attempt to resolve differences of opinion? How do you get along sexually together? What is the communication like between you? How do you get along with family, children, and friends? How compatible are you as a couple? How do you feel you compare to other couples? Both spouses are given an opportunity to respond to each question and their style of responding is observed allowing comparison to other couples who respond to this rather structured section.

FEEDBACK, EVALUATION, THERAPY CONTRACT

The interviewer now has about 10 minutes to provide feedback about the presenting problem, the relationship of the presenting problem to issues of spouse selection, and the influence of the parents' marriage, issues from the history and the current relationship. The feedback is usually positive and negative. For example, the problem of persistent unresolved arguments was present during courtship, but you believed it would stop after your marriage in spite of growing up with arguments on both sides of the family. Currently arguments over your marriage roles persist in spite of a lot of affection, compatibility, and commitment. The couple are asked whether they agree or disagree with these observations.

Next I explain the theory of marital intimacy to the couple. I explain that my experience and research suggest that couples often feel a lack of closeness and although this does not necessarily cause their arguments, sessions in which I help them disclose more of their thoughts about their relationship may reduce the arguments in their relationship. I outline that in general I will try to help them understand why they argue by exploring their theories of the influence of their parents' marriage, their motivations for choosing their spouse, and their ideas about the relationship.

I am still somewhat surprised that well over 9 out of 10 couples at least tentatively accept this model and agree to participate in 10 one-hour sessions of cognitive self-disclosure. I describe the format of the sessions to the couple. (I will describe the format for the reader in the next chapter.) I ask the couple if they would be willing to complete three self-report questionnaires for me before the next session and get 100% return and give them feedback of their results in the second session. They complete the General Health Questionnaire, a measure of symptoms of nonpsychotic emotional illness, the Locke–Wallace Marital Adjustment Scale, and the Waring Intimacy Questionnaire (Goldberg, 1972; Locke & Wallace, 1959; Waring, 1984).

What about the couples who do not accept the theory or agree to a treatment contract? Some couples do not wish to participate in self-disclosure. Some couples want specific advice about what to do about specific impasses or opinions about whether the marriage is viable, specific prescriptions of recommended behavioral changes, or a focus on the here and now. Occasionally couples will question the importance of current difficulties to parental intimacy or marital choice, but often they are willing to give the therapy a chance. I try to give other couples what they have expected or refer them to colleagues.

Finally, I ask the couple their opinions about the initial assessment. The majority disclose that it was not what they expected, that the disclosures were interesting, that they learned things they had not known, and that they are hopeful about the therapy. Often they express amazement about how similar their problems are to those of their parents. Of course some people have been dissatisfied and through direct and indirect feedback, I hear that spouses perceive that I did not give the presenting problem enough time or did not seem to take it "seriously" or that I did not seem supportive enough of their point of view.

HOW THE FAMILY INTERVIEW DIFFERS

With the children present, the session begins with asking all family members their theories about why the presenting problem exists. Obviously, this takes a bit more time and the opinions and beliefs are often surprisingly inconsistent.

The children then offer their observations along with their parents' about their grandparents' marriages. The children passively listen while the parents describe their attraction, dating, courtship. The parents are told to let me know if they do not wish to disclose something. Often the children have never heard their parents describe their courtship. The family life history follows and then the children passively listen as the eight intimacy factors are explored. Finally, family issues of discipline, home atmosphere, and family recreation may be added as needed. The same theory is presented to all family members with, for example, Johnny's truancy being related to the intimacy factor. The children are told they will not be invited to the 10 sessions.

COMMENTS ABOUT ASSESSMENT

The assessment is designed to introduce the couple or family to cognitive self-disclosure in a structured format. No feelings or nonverbal communications or behaviors are commented on or focused on. The interviewer, however, notes the *content* being discussed when a family member *reacts* rather than *responds* as Bowen (1975) has described. When a spouse reacts with anger or tears to a specific content area, this often represents the core conflict issue of deficient intimacy. Feelings are suppressed because *most* affect in initial assessments is negative and produces distance. The interview focuses on essential cognitive schemas which influence the quality and quantity of intimacy. These are 1) the parents'—and grandparents'—quality and quantity of intimacy; 2) the conscious reasons for marital choice; and 3) the issues of marital interaction.

In the remainder of the chapter I describe the initial assessments of three couples: 1) a couple with a relationship problem; 2) a couple in which each presents dissatisfaction with the spouse's character; and 3) a couple where one spouse has a psychiatric diagnosis. These descriptions are, of course, composites to protect confidentiality, but they begin to give clinical life and meaning to the following chapter on therapy.

CASE 1—A RELATIONSHIP PROBLEM

This couple were referred because they were drifting apart and having increasingly bitter and frequent arguments. They had been married for eight years and had two daughters, ages 7 and 4. He was a professional man who traveled extensively. She was at home with the two girls, which she enjoyed.

When asked their theories of why the drifting apart and arguments began, she identified her bitterness after the birth of the second child that he spent little time at home. His temper became more evident, and he stopped being a companion, leaving her feeling lonely. He stated that after the birth of both children he found his wife boring and preoccupied with the children and domestic life.

They next disclosed that they had met through her work as a secretary/receptionist. He was one of many businessmen who reported through her office. She said that she found him physically attractive, mature, and assertive, whereas her previous boy friends had been passive. She thought he was married at the time they first dated. He corrected her and said his previous wife and he had already separated and he found her physically attractive and pleasant. He revealed that her parents had not been pleased with their courtship. They both agreed that they found they had some mutual interests in music and both enjoyed dining and entertainment related to professional interests. When asked about his previous marriage, he revealed that both he and his wife were ambitious, career-oriented people whose business resulted in frequent separations. An opportunity for his wife led to her moving and his decision not to accompany her. He acknowledged that they had had difficulties in resolving differences of opinion but separated on good terms with no children. She revealed that she had not thought about why his previous marriage had failed. Her decision to date a married man was motivated in part by rebellion.

They spontaneously disclosed that they had separated after six months of courtship when she learned that he was seeing somebody else at a time when arguments in their relationship about commitment were leading them to reconsider their relationship. They both had romances during this three-month hiatus and spontaneously got back together when he called. They both denied jealousy or bitterness about these transient romances.

He described his parents' marriage as poor. He attributed this to his father, who was intimidating and bad-tempered. Verbal and physical abuse of his mother and siblings had occurred and there had been two brief separations. He was not close to his family, and avoided visits or contacts. She described her parents' marriage as good, but said that her mother had been overinvolved with her as an only child. She described her mother as placating and always trying to please everyone, including her father, who was a private man. There was a suggestion the father had had an affair.

They described their first few years of marriage as being happy. Frequent weekly separations were not upsetting, but he said he was bored and lonely at times on the road. They enjoyed an active social life when together and when alone she spent considerable time with her family.

The birth of the children was planned and both spouses were pleased. She left work and devoted her time to the children. He, as mentioned, was not as comfortable with his role as father. There had been no affairs or external distressing relationships, although she found his family difficult to deal with and he found his mother-in-law to be somewhat intrusive.

Both clearly stated they were committed to the relationship and wanted to see it improve. They agreed expression of affection had been worse since the arguments and that she tended to be more expressive. They both agreed that resolving differences of opinion frequently led to arguments and that his temper was expressed more frequently. He suggested that he generally preferred to keep his thoughts to himself and was not a good listener at home because he felt tired from his work, which involved listening to clients. She disclosed that she enjoyed conversation and was a bit of a mind reader. They both agreed their sexual relationship was good. They felt their relationship to friends and extended family was positive except for continued turmoil with his parents. They felt good about themselves as individuals and a couple. They still had mutual goals, values, and activities.

I suggested that their lack of intimacy was probably related to an inability to resolve differences of opinion which had been present during courtship and which both had observed and experienced in their families of origin with his overt and hers covert. They both accepted that

10 sessions to facilitate self-disclosure might be helpful. He wanted to know what my success rate was so I gave him an article to read. She was a bit disappointed that I was not going to tell them something to do to improve things in the next week.

CASE 2—A MARRIAGE OF A HYSTERICAL AND OBSESSIONAL CHARACTER

This couple's major complaints were that she saw him as boring, unaffectionate, and no fun and he saw her as unpredictable, emotional, and demanding. When asked why she believed she had picked a boring, unaffectionate man, she said that when they met in high school he was serious, mature, and not "after only one thing," like the other boys. He said that she was outgoing, sociable, and attractive. They had been married for six years and had one child aged 6 years. Both stated that if it was not for their daughter they would have seriously considered separation.

They met when he was a senior in high school and she was two years behind. She was a blind date for an important school dance. She had just broken up with an older boy friend who was working and of whom her parents disapproved. He had had no serious romances and few dates. She found him serious and square at first, but he found her very attractive and sexy. They began dating regularly and just before graduating she discovered she was pregnant. Both said they had been thinking of getting married anyway, but he mentioned he had been considering going away to college.

She disclosed that her parents had divorced when she was 5 years old and she did not know why the divorce occurred. She knew little about her natural father. She was the oldest of three children. Her mother, with whom she lived, had remarried when the patient was 10 and they had had a stormy relationship, but she thought they cared for each other. She had not gotten along with her stepfather, whom she viewed as excessively strict. They both liked her husband from the beginning, but she was happy to get away from the bickering at home. He disclosed that his parents had a good stable marriage, but she interrupted to say they were not very demonstrative and he agreed. He was the youngest of five children and he did not tell his parents about the pregnancy, but he was sure they knew about this event. He believed his parents had been very supportive of his professional development, both financially and with encouragement.

They both described their wedding as fun, but she expressed disappointment that she did not have a honeymoon due to his work and lack of money. They were both happy with the birth of their daughter, but she had a difficult and exhausting labor and delivery. She lost interest in sex gradually and disclosed that she had never been able to reach orgasm with her husband. They had talked about seeing a counselor for this difficulty, but never got around to making an appointment. He disclosed that she had had a brief affair after two years of marriage and he was very bitter and had considered separation but decided to stay for the sake of his daughter. They had had many arguments at that time and once he had lost control and hit her. She developed a number of physical complaints and a preoccupation with her health leading to a hysterectomy two years ago, after which she was very depressed. He withdrew even more after this and although the arguments stopped they were leading largely separate lives. The event which precipitated the referral was a job offer in another city where she did not want to move, leading to talk of a possible separation.

They said that they were committed to trying to improve the relationship, but if the counseling was not helpful, they would consider separation. Both agreed that although they cared for one another there was no expression of affection. They agreed that they could talk and listen quite well about practical details, but they avoided talking about their private thoughts and feelings or about their relationship. They agreed they were incompatible: he enjoyed quiet intellectual pursuits and she enjoyed people and entertainment. Both agreed their sexual relationship had always been poor and there had been no intercourse for over one year. They had few friends as a couple, spent time with their parents on only special occasions, and were preoccupied with their daughter. Both felt poorly that their marriage was not close. They no longer had any fights.

I pointed out to them that their lack of closeness was related to their motivations to pick someone who they felt had qualities lacking in themselves. Without greater understanding of their own motivations for this type of choice and the influence of their parents' marriages and the pregnancy on their choices, it would be difficult to resolve their difficulties. They agreed with this and accepted the 10-session treatment contract. I advised them to postpone decisions regarding a separation until the end of the sessions.

CASE 3—A PSYCHOSOMATIC PROBLEM

This couple was referred because the wife had persistent migraine headaches which had failed to respond to medical treatments and had had two admissions related to alcohol abuse, feelings of suicide, and depression.

They met while students at a college where he was a graduate teaching assistant with her in his laboratory. She described being attracted to him because of his knowledge and self-confident attitude. He described her as attractive and said he enjoyed the attention she paid him. The relationship started as a student–tutor relationship until she invited him to a party.

She described her parents' marriage as cold, sterile, and aloof. She disclosed that her father was perceived as a locally important personage who often belittled his wife and children. He described his parents' marriage as stable and said it "seemed" good. He reported that he had very little contact with his parents because he found his mother overinvolved with his career.

Their courtship was somewhat stormy with her having temper tantrums when his work and research took precedence over their social life. She also felt disappointed that she was not doing well academically. He said that she was miserable and he felt he married her to rescue her from her disillusionment.

When they first were married, the pattern continued of arguments over lack of time together because of career interest. There were also sexual problems including premature ejaculation and frigidity. She mentioned sexual dissatisfaction once to her family physician, but nothing further was done. She spent considerable time looking after her ailing mother.

She became pregnant about three years later and had a very difficult pregnancy and labor. She regretted not being able to continue her studies. She developed headaches shortly after the delivery and the couple lost interest in sex. The baby was very colicky and she became depressed and began drinking. He began to spend even less time at home.

The relationship settled down after two to three years when she started back to school and their child entered day-care.

There was little affection between them and he verbalized that if she did not control her drinking, he was leaving. They believed they were compatible and seldom argued. Their sex life was poor and they seldom talked about their relationship. They had few friends and she was devoted to her son, but he had little time for the boy.

Both agreed that their lack of closeness might be related to the perpetuation of headaches and drinking.

4

The Technique

Cognitive Family Therapy begins with an evaluation interview with the couple or with all family members present, as described in Chapter 3. The focus of the evaluation is to elicit each spouse's "theory" of why the presenting problem or symptom appeared. The children's cognitive explanation of why the family is not functioning optimally and the couples' theories regarding their parents' relationships are elicited. A developmental history of the couples' courtship, marriage, and family, as well as their parents' marriage, is obtained.

The interviewer asks only "why" or "theory" questions and avoids and suppresses feelings and/or behavioral interpretations or confrontation. The interviewer evaluates the eight dimensions of marital intimacy from the Victoria Hospital Intimacy Interview: affection, cohesion, expressiveness, compatibility, conflict resolution, sexuality, autonomy, and identity. This facilitates the identification of the couple's strengths as well as the dimensions which are determining the lack of intimacy (Waring, 1981).

The interviewer then explains to the couple or the entire family the theory on which the therapy is based and the couples are offered 10 one-hour sessions to increase their intimacy (or improve one of the specific eight areas of intimate relationships) and, as a result, improve family functioning and the symptomatology of the presenting patient. Then the specific rules and behaviors of the self-disclosure sessions are outlined and negotiation and discussion follow until a specific treatment contract is made.

Only the marital couple is involved in the sessions. The session begins with the therapist stating, "We are here to understand why you are not close." As the therapy proceeds, the session begins with the major "why" question unanswered from the previous session. The couple may talk only to the therapist in an alternate pattern during the sessions. No feeling or behavior is identified, confronted, or interpreted. The couple alternates in talking about any biographical material they think is relevant to answering the "why" question. The therapist in a standardized manner asks the other spouse, "What were you thinking while your spouse was talking?," thus facilitating cognitive self-disclosure. The therapist may also ask a spouse's theory on the question the other spouse cannot answer. The therapist may share his or her cognitive theories. The therapist does not use interpretation or cognitive restructuring to clarify material disclosed to current conflict. When the couple understands a particular "why" question, a more sophisticated "why" question becomes apparent.

Although this description may sound like a tedious process for the therapist to conduct in this stereotyped format, the material and revelations are surprisingly fascinating.

Clinical skills develop through the perceptiveness of the therapist's "why" questions.

Our couple with an interpersonal problem of drifting apart is the first example.

T: What's your theory about why you have drifted apart as a couple?

W: George refuses to accept my point of view about anything!

T: Your theory is that your drifting apart was due to your husband not respecting your opinions?

W: Yes.

T: Why did you select a man who doesn't respect your opinions?

W: He wasn't that way when we met. He was very passive when we met.

T: What is your theory about why he changed?

W: He changed after the children were born. I don't know why.

T: George, what were you thinking when your wife was talking?

H: I was thinking that Alice wants me to agree with all her decisions.

T: What's your theory about why your wife wants total consensus?

H: She wants to control the kids' behavior.

T: Why did you marry someone who appears to want control of decisions?

H: She always knew what she wanted and I liked that at first because I didn't.

One can observe the process of self-disclosure commencing as the wife begins to think about her reasons for marrying a passive man and the husband begins to think about why he did not know what he wanted. Both spouses will now be exploring their own motives for spouse selection, it is hoped with some objectivity provided by the passage of time. Now each spouse can be a resource regarding observations and explanations of these earlier motives.

T: (to wife) What were you thinking while your spouse was talking?

W: I was thinking that I didn't know what I wanted as clearly as George thinks. I was pretty confused.

T: What's your theory of what was causing your confusion?

W: My mother was considering separating because of my father's affair and I was confused about who I could trust.

T: What's your theory of why your father had an affair?

W: I don't know. He was spending a lot of time with his secretary, who was a young woman. I don't know.

T: (to husband) What were you thinking while your wife was talking?

H: I think he was tired of being taken for granted at home. At least that's what he told me once.

T: What's your theory about why spouses are taken for granted?

We are now a long way from the original focus on drifting apart in the present to explaining reasons for an affair which occurred in the wife's parents' marriage and the question of men being taken for granted.

Our second couple involved a male patient with a compulsive character and a wife with hysterical character features.

T: What's your theory about why you picked someone you considered boring and unemotional?

W: I thought he was stable and secure when we met.

T: Why do you think you needed stability and security?

W: I was very insecure at the time.

T: Insecure?

W: I was unhappy at home and my father was always on my case. I wanted to be popular and would do anything to have a boy friend.

T: (to husband) What's your theory about why you picked a woman you consider impulsive and inconsistent?

H: Well, she seemed to be so much fun when we met.

T: What's your theory of why you weren't having any fun?

H: I felt under a lot of pressure at the time to do well at school.

T: Why did you have to do well at school?

H: It seemed to be something my family would be proud of.

Here again the process of self-disclosure has the husband focusing on why he felt compelled to seek academic success while she is thinking about feelings of insecurity. The couple is already focusing on different expressions of personal insecurity in their relationship. This mutual compatibility regarding insecurity later led to the couple having a premarital pregnancy. One would not be surprised if the parents' marriages might also have had problems with insecurity.

Finally, consider the beginning of therapy with the psychosomatic couple.

T: What is your theory of why your headaches and drinking have continued?

W: I think it was because the headaches kept me from doing things outside the house.

T: Go on.

W: I think that I was unhappy just looking after the house and the children.

T: What's your theory of why you were dissatisfied with your role at home?

W: I felt useless and wanted to do something worthwhile.

T: (to husband) What is your theory of why your wife's headaches persisted?

H: I don't think I noticed at the time because I was so busy.

T: Why didn't you notice?

H: She didn't talk to me about the headaches.

THERAPIST'S TECHNIQUES

This approach enhances marital intimacy through facilitating *cognitive* self-disclosure. This section describes what you *say* and *do* as a therapist. Everything you say and do is designed to facilitate the spouses' saying "I think . . ." or "I am . . ." All behaviors, interactions, and feelings which reduce the possibility of one spouse revealing his or her thoughts with the other spouse listening attentively are to be suppressed. (This should be explained to the couple at the onset and forms a significant part of the treatment contract.)

Although the techniques were designed to ensure standardization of therapist behavior, you will still have considerable flexibility to follow the couple's themes. The therapist can ask questions stimulated by cognitive curiosity providing these questions produce further cognitive self-disclosure.

Supervision of sessions is provided to students who utilize audiotapes to ensure standardization. These tapes assist in helping students develop increasing skill in the types of questions asked.

Explanation of Sessions and Treatment Contract

Therapy starts with the following statement: "We will be meeting for 10 sessions over a 10-week period. During the sessions I will ask you a series of questions designed to help you understand why your relationship is not as close as you both wish. During the sessions you agree not to interrupt your spouse while he (or she) attempts to answer the questions. I will turn to the other spouse in an alternating pattern and ask 'What were you thinking?' The questions will be about your marriage and your parents' and grandparents' relationships. If there are interruptions, I will terminate the session. Between sessions you may talk about material from the sessions and you may wish to contact relatives for information. If you both agree, we can commence the session or I will answer any questions you may want to ask."

Initiation of First and Subsequent Interviews

The first question addressed to the female spouse is "What is your theory of why your marriage is distant?" or "What is your theory of why your husband drinks excessively?" or "What is your theory of why you had an affair?" The specific question about the specific presenting problem should be repeated to the other spouse.

Self-disclosure can be facilitated by nondirective questions such as "Go on," "Uh huh," "Tell me more" until the patient says "I don't know" or three to five minutes go by.

The first question of each subsequent session should be the last unanswered question of the previous session. The therapist should always write down the final question of each session for reference.

In the first case, the self-disclosure in the assessment interview has already introduced the theme of the wife's belief that her efforts are not worthwhile and the husband's avoidance of personal relationships.

I will use transcripts from therapy sessions with a couple who had persistent arguments to demonstrate response to specific therapist interventions previously described during the course of therapy. The first clinical example illustrates explaining the theory and making a treatment contract followed by the initiation of the therapy session. The details and names are altered to respect confidentiality.

T: The last time we were here what we agreed to do was try to sort of play a detective game and understand the arguments and battle for control that perhaps go on behind the arguments that keep you from being as close as you'd like. As I mentioned, the only rule is that you can't talk while the other person's talking. You can't interrupt. Ladies get to go first. What's your theory about what the battle for control is about?

W: If I knew what the battle for control was all about, I think we could probably have worked it out ourselves.

T: Em hm.

W: That's the major problem. We don't seem to know what is causing so many of our arguments lately.

T: Do you have any theories or assumptions?

W: Initially Bill was not too content at what he was doing.

T: Em hm.

W: He was unhappy with his job. I was very content and I think that that started causing problems. I think that maybe that was part of it or the initial thing that started it. I'm sure there were a lot of other things that were on the way to adding to it.

T: And what's your theory of how that would result in the two of you having a battle for control? (long pause) Well, I guess in general you were happy in what you were doing and you think your husband was unhappy in what he was doing. I think that that could cause envy as one possibility. What do you think of that theory?

W: I think that is a fair assumption that it was a bit of envy on his part.

T: Have there ever been issues of envy in your family?

W: I honestly can't think of any. You're talking in relation to Bill?

T: No. I'm talking in relationship to your family. Mother, father, and your sister.

W: Em hm.

T: That's it.

W: Mother, father, and sister?

T: Any issues of envy in your family?

W: Oh yes. Lots.

T: Tell me about that.

W: Ah—

T: Who's envious of whom?

W: I think my sister and I . . . have been envious of each other at different times.

T: And what have you been envious of in her and what's she been envious of in you?

W: She was always the good one in school. I was always envious of the fact that she never had to do any work and I had to work to get every mark I got. Um. I think she was envious of me because I was the gregarious one. She was very quiet and withdrawn. I was open and I was always the one that struck up new acquaintances. Did different things.

T: And what were you thinking about while your wife was talking?

H: I think that was the reason I was smiling because I don't think she's got a whole lot to be envious of her sister. That's my answer. Her sister's got a lot more to be envious of than perhaps Mary.

T: What's your theory about who provided the payoff for success in those areas?

H: Mary's mother's attention was won by her and her father's attention was won by her sister.

T: So dad liked school performance and mom liked sociability?

H: Ah, yeah. I'd say that's probably correct.

T: What did you think about my theory about envy?

H: I think that it was very true five years ago. Our situation has changed since last time we were here. When I came here I worked so all of a sudden I'm without employment.

T: Makes you less envious or more envious?

H: At this stage it probably won't affect us financially, it's no burden. It's kind of like a holiday. Ah. Two months from now I think it will be very different. I mean I'm not the type to just be around. So I'm not envious of

her position because she's not teaching anyway. But I
. . . in the past, yes.

T: And in your family, was envy an issue?

H: I really don't know. You know being an only child
and that I can't really relate to that.

T: And you didn't have any—

H: I think I was jealous of my father sometimes.

T: Why were you envious of him?

H: Because of the person he still is. He is a fairly dynamic
type of little guy.

Comment. In attempting to understand their battle for
control, the couple are exploring a theory related to envy.
This idea may or may not be true, but in the process they
are disclosing their ideas about the role of envy in their
families and later address the issue of envy in their parents'
marriages.

Facilitating Cognitive Self-Disclosure

"What were you thinking while your spouse was talking?"
This question is frequently repeated and is the *cornerstone*
of facilitating cognitive self-disclosure.

First you should assist the spouses in clarifying their
thoughts, beliefs, attitudes, and opinions. The husband
may say "I feel my wife is exaggerating." You should help
them recognize that this is not a "feeling" but an opinion.
Many people use the word "feel" when they are revealing
thought. A spouse may respond "I wasn't thinking anything, I was just listening." A typical response would be
"What do you think you heard?" A spouse may comment
on the other spouse's behavior or affective tone such as

"I think she sounds angry!" A typical response might be "Why do you think you married someone who sounds angry?"

The therapist should find as many ways to encourage cognitive self-disclosure as possible. The questions may initiate thoughts which appear unrelated to what the spouse has revealed. The focus should always be exploration of the thoughts about themselves or assistance to the spouses in understanding the relationship.

The pattern of facilitating self-disclosure is initiated by the question "What were you thinking?"

T: What were you thinking while your wife was talking?

H: I find it believable, but envy between us is something that we've never discussed. I didn't think we had too many secrets from each other.

W: It's not a secret. *(Wife interrupts; this breaking of a therapy rule signals an emotional reaction to an important issue.)*

T: You'll get your chance.

W: Well, OK—it's just that there are things coming out that perhaps I thought in the past I might have heard already.

T: Well, I think two things that have come out so far are that there's been an issue of envy between girls, for at least two generations.

H: It still exists.

T: And there's been an issue about sex and secretiveness and shame about it for at least two generations. So let's find out about sex and envy in your family for a couple of generations.

H: I don't remember my parents being overly affectionate. I don't remember, you know, just in the morning and I suppose a kiss at night I remember. I don't remember anything in regard to the sex relationship. I didn't walk in or anything like that. It was fairly understated.

T: And what do you know about their courtship?

H: I don't know a lot about it. It's never really been discussed. I thought that my mother and I talked about just about everything.

T: Em hm.

H: My father and I were not and still are not particularly . . . close, but ah . . .

T: Tell me a bit about that. What's your theory about why the two of you aren't close?

H: Why the two of us aren't?

T: Em hm. Your father and . . .

H: I ah . . . I'm resentful of him. To a certain extent.

T: Tell me about that.

H: He's a fairly interesting man. He's accomplished quite a bit. Well, I might be envious of him I'm sure.

Comment. This example from later in the first session demonstrates the process of self-disclosure as the husband begins to examine his observations of his parents' marriage.

Clarification

After the spouse has disclosed what he or she is thinking, the therapist may help the spouse clarify theories, beliefs, and values by nondirective questioning or relabeling or rephrasing thoughts.

Nondirective questions include "Tell me more about your thoughts" and "Could you explain more about your beliefs."

Rephrasing involves putting the patient's thoughts into brief and clearer words not unlike a précis. "You think women are inconsistent." or "You think you were motivated by greed."

In the second session with the same couple, I start with the question unanswered from the previous session.

T: What's your theory about the envy that we heard about last week?

W: The envy's there. I'm not sure why it's there. Like none of us have any reason to be envious of any of the other people in the family. I mean everybody's doing fairly well. Nobody's struggling. Nobody's really, you know, down and out. I don't see any reason for the envy to be there.

T: But it is.

W: It is.

T: Last week we heard that it was mainly between the ladies, you and your sister, and his mother and her two men.

W: Em hm. The men in my family. The man, my father, is very, very quiet. He doesn't show emotions at all. Basically a very quiet, withdrawn man. My uncle's the same way. He's very quiet. He just sits back and lets the women run the show.

T: What's your theory about that? Why is he a quiet, withdrawn man?

W: Because his wife is so dominant. Their wives are so dominant that they're forced to.

T: It's hopeless?

W: Yeah. They put up with it for so many years. It is a totally hopeless family. You can't change that. Not at this stage of the game.

T: So what's your theory to date? *Did they pick dominating women or did they become passive during the interaction of being married?*

W: It's hard to say since I didn't know my mom back then or my aunt previously, but I think you can learn to become dominant.

T: Em hm.

W: If you are forced to do things on your own and forced to do a lot of things within a marriage, then you know, I think you could learn to become that way. I don't know if they learned to be dominant or the mate they chose was dominant.

Comment. The therapist attempts to help the wife explore her ideas about whether dominant women are selected or created.

Redirection

A wife may say "I think I was wrong to marry because I was lonely." The therapist asks the husband, "What were you thinking while your wife was talking?" The husband responds, "I was thinking about the parking meter."

The therapist should initially use clarification to understand the parking meter thought, but if this fails, the therapist should redirect the husband back to the core question for the couple. "What did you think about your wife's thought about loneliness as a motive for marriage?" or "Why did you pick a lonely woman to marry?"

This is the same couple in their third session.

T: So what was the rivalry between you and your sister?

W: I honestly am not sure because we were treated equally. Whatever one got, the other one got. There were no two ways about that . . . I may have had to wait a year longer to get what Joan had because she was the older one and she got it first, but we were always treated very, very much equally.

T: Whose favorite were you?

W: That's where the rivalry came in. My sister told me about that a year ago on the telephone. She really shocked me. I don't know if I'd been sick or what. I'd had pneumonia or something and I didn't want to tell my parents because they would just get worried and then my mom wants to come down to London and baby me for a week and I thought no I didn't need that. A lot of what I needed was just to stay in bed and relax and Joan said something to the effect that you know mom and dad both always loved you best and ah . . .

T: Em hm.

W: Typical . . . You know if they find out that you're sick they're really going to get sick themselves. They'll be worried sick about you so don't tell them.

T; So she believed that you were the favorite?

W: Yes.

T: (redirection) And the description of your husband in terms of my theory that things run in families like a sexual grudge. You were the sexy one, the attractive one, the personable one.

W: I was the outgoing one. She was very reserved and quiet. Joan is pretty. She's really pretty.

T: Did you start to date before her?

W: No. There's only a year and a half difference. We pretty well started at the same time only because my mom was in Europe with her grandmother at the time. I was 15½ just going on 16 and I was told that I was not allowed to go out on dates until I hit 16. Because my mom was gone and my dad was more easy to get along with he let me go out. So Joan and I pretty well went out. I think our first date was double-dating.

T: So it was your mother's fears that you girls shouldn't go out because you . . .

W: Oh, I . . .

T: might get carried away?

W: Yeah. I think my father had the same fears, but he was so quiet and reserved that he never really let it show. Plus the fact that my mother was handling it just fine by herself so he let her continue it and then she went to Europe. He was so busy with the business and everything he said sure you know you can go out.

T: So was there a sexual grudge between the two of you? A stolen boy friend?

W: No. No. None of that. No, she always, Joan dates good-looking fellows. There was never you know my dating her boy friends or vice versa. Um . . . I was more popular at parties and we did a lot of things together. We had a lot of the same friends.

T: So who made love first?

W: She did.

T: She did?

W: Yeah.

T: Tell me about that.

W: Well, I'm not sure about the whole thing. She never really told me all the details, but we were in Europe when she found a guy she really liked.

T: So your mother's worst fears came true?

W: Yes.

Comment. The therapist redirects the wife to a theory proposed by her husband that the envy in his family was related to sexual themes.

Nondirective Questions

Therapists should use nondirective questions as much as possible to encourage cognitive self-disclosure for approximately three to five minutes. These questions should be used as much as possible because the core of the therapy is the couple's self-disclosure (the process) rather than the therapist's ideas of what issues are important.

Here are the same people at the beginning of the fourth session.

T: We were wondering about whether sexual issues might be related to envy or power conflicts. Tell me more about sex.

W: It's been good the last little while, but I get mad when he gets really demanding.

T: And what does he demand that you get mad about?

W: I get mad when you know after having made love it's over and he's thinking about when he can do it again. Like there's never enough.

T: Em hm. Remind me. Did you tell me you're not able to have orgasms? *Tell me more about that.*

W: I feel quite contented after making love. I was very distressed about the lack of orgasms a couple of years ago I guess.

T: *Tell me about that.* Why were you distressed?

W: It's not a good feeling to find out that you're not "normal." That there's something a bit different from the norm.

T: Em hm.

W: And that's a put down to ego and everything. I was distressed about it, but I've come around to the train of thought where well as long as I am enjoying it that's all that really matters. May I . . .

T: Did you go see somebody about it?

W: Um . . . Yeah. I saw . . . yeah, I did, I saw a couple of doctors. I've just been in and out of doctors' offices so many times.

H: No, but that wasn't true. What about Dr. Smith? *(Husband's interruption suggests that he is reacting to an important conflict.)*

W: That's what I was thinking about. Dr. Smith and that.

T: What did he tell you?

W: We . . . didn't get into it with him. We were supposed to go back for more appointments, but that would have to be school time and I couldn't get the time off school.

T: Em hm.

W: There was just no way and he couldn't take us during March break so I think the first session we had with him was really excellent and it would have been quite worthwhile to go back and see him again, but there's just no way we could fit it in. He doesn't work evenings and he was spending the time with their kids which is natural for March break.

T: Does your mother have orgasms?

W: Oh. I don't know.

T: Never asked her?

W: We never talked about sex.

T: Why not?

W: It was just a topic that was never discussed.

T: It was certainly discussed in terms of prohibitions about it.

W: Oh. Yes. It was always. There was always a negative connotation or association with sex.

Comment. Nondirective questions allow discussion of a very sensitive topic related to the relationship of the couple's sexual dysfunction to the power conflict. This couple's sexual dysfunction is also related to the parents' relationship.

Parents' Marriages

The therapist should encourage the couple to think about their parents' marriages when there are questions they are unable to answer. A spouse may say "I don't know why we argue so frequently."

The therapist should encourage any effort on the part of the couple to understand (response) as opposed to blame (react) the motivations of their parents in their marriage. This may involve direct contact for information with relatives.

The same couple in session 5 follows.

T: Tell me a bit about what you didn't know.
W: Well, I didn't realize my great-grandparents were American. Um . . . that surprised me. I thought my parents were the first ones that ever left but they weren't. We drove down to the Oregon coast and we saw my uncle and mother's brother down there and heard a lot about their family for two days. They are really messed up badly. I think what I learned more than anything is my family's pretty messed up. There's a lot of problems in every single family. Our part of the family . . . my

parents, my sister, and I seem to be the most sane of the whole bunch I think.

T: Em hm.

W: I never thought of . . .

T: What was messed up that you found out about there?

W: Well my aunt had died and my cousin, her son, disappeared! His sister knows where he is but he wants no part of her. She just calls him once every six months to make sure he's still alive. Even then it's why are you calling me, why do you keep bugging me, just leave me alone, I don't want to talk to you or anybody else. Sally ripped off her father for 50,000 dollars. This is a brother and sister in the same family. She put him into bankruptcy and he drinks a lot. He's OK now but the whole family is just sore. For two days I was in the middle of it. Both trying to defend themselves and their positions.

T: What were you thinking while your wife was talking?

H: Well, I saw the same thing down there that I saw in Toronto. There is a tremendous rivalry, jealousy, whatever you want to call it. It's just incredible. I've just never seen anything like it. Mary's uncle is a very dynamic old man who has done very, very well. You could write a book on his life. He lost his wife in a fire when he was younger, and he's been bankrupt and it just goes on and on. You know he just hates his son-in-law with a passion because he drives as nice a car as he does—they both have Cadillacs, the same color, this type of thing. We went for a ride in the Cadillac and he says to me, Whose Cadillac do you like, is his bigger than mine? It's not really that he has a lot of money, but he's putting on the act. He's secure, but his business isn't so spectacular. He's supposed to tell her mother that her brother's quite successful. But the hate that's between him and his daughter and his son-in-law. The son-in-law has a store maybe five times as big as his. He started his son-in-law off in business. They all hate him and I don't particularly like him as a person, but he's no fool. I think that they hate him for that. But . . . like the pressure between them, the friction, it's just incredible. I . . . I just . . . you know we were both quite relieved to leave. I told everybody off. But I was quite relieved to just get out of this pressure cooker. We had problems with them when we got married five years ago. All of a sudden when we have to go start seeing the cousins, it wasn't the best experience for any of us really. Especially for Mary.

T: What did you discover about your family?

H: I think my father had no doubts about leaving Scotland as quickly as he did when he was 38. Certainly he was a little upset that his mother didn't come to bid him farewell as such. She never said goodbye, obviously she was a little bit . . . I didn't realize it . . . perturbed. That was basically it.

T: Your grandmother was unhappy enough not to—

H: Very much so. Yes . . . she . . . that was basically the end of the relationship between my father and her. My mother was not overly impressed with my grandmother.

T: So. You do something in your family that people disagree with and they psychologically disown you. What were you thinking?

W: I was thinking about Scott's dad and all the stories he was telling us. It sounded to me that he wasn't even an afterthought, he just happened. He was totally unexpected. The third little boy. I think that if he had been born a little girl, then he would have been loved as dearly as the two other boys were. He was never really accepted by either one of his parents.

T: So he grew up feeling unwanted?

W: I think so. I get that impression. A couple of times there were even tears in his eyes when he was talking. He was talking about leaving the inheritance. And he really doesn't care. He really doesn't. He's not that type of man. He's done very well on his own, but it's still another little slight along with you know with six years of life where the other two sons, his two brothers, each got a nice gift from the grandfather. Their father left a gold watch or a gold coin or something along the way and he was always left out. They never really acknowledged the fact that he had been born and was there. I felt that there was a lot of . . . feeling . . . I can't . . . I don't know whether it was resentment or just sadness. I think it's more sadness that it has to be that way and that's the way he had been treated.

Comment. The wife discloses issues of envy in her family and he discloses issues of abandonment and neglect in his family. In later sessions this couple, who were infertile, were asked if envy between them or fear of neglecting a child might be related to their sexual dysfunction or infertility.

Grandparents, Friends, and Other Couples

A spouse may say "I don't know why I married an alcoholic." The therapist should ask, in order, "Do you have any theories about why your mother, grandmother, sister, friends, whoever, married an alcoholic?" The therapist may ask "Do you have any theories about why some women marry alcoholics?" The therapist may suggest general reasons if the spouse is unable, perhaps the spouse didn't recognize the alcoholism or thought the drinking would stop after the marriage or considered the prospective spouse entertaining while intoxicated.

The following is a session discussing the couple's grandparents' marriages.

T: Tell us about your homelife.

H: My mother's father was very much like my father's father. He was the strong, dominant, quick-tempered one, which I didn't know.

T: Em hm.

H: And my mother's mother was very much more passive and low-keyed. That's about all there is.

T: How did your mother feel about his quick temper?

H: Well, she is a little quick-tempered too. So you know she comes by it honestly.

T: Tell me about your mother's quick temper.

H: She has high blood pressure and we don't see her that often but she tends to get wound up fairly quickly.

T: High blood pressure is sometimes thought by people to result from their blood boiling.

H: She just seems to get aggravated fairly quickly about small things sometimes. We don't see it as much but I believe it to be true. Talking to my father.

T: And what did she get irritated at him about? And quick-tempered at him about?

H: Just being him I think. I don't remember her being quick-tempered when I was younger, but I have noticed it in the last few years.

T: Em hm.

H: It comes and goes. It doesn't seem to affect him too much.

Comment. The husband is now disclosing about the expression of anger in his parents' marriage, which is parallel to the pattern of expression of anger in his marriage. Did he select a quick-tempered woman?

In session 6 the couple deals with friends or other couples.

T: What's your theory about why he married a lady who goes on guilt trips?

W: I have absolutely no idea.

T: You don't know why someone would marry someone who goes on guilt trips?

W: Perhaps it makes them feel more superior because they're not on guilt trips?

T: From what you've told me so far, my theory would be to make them feel more secure. Since the ultimate threat seems to be that a spouse will leave. Maybe people on guilt trips don't leave as easy.

W: No. (long pause) True.

T: The reverse of that is why did you marry someone who wants to feel so important?

W: I don't know.

T: What were you thinking about while your wife was talking?

H: I don't think I like that. Maybe I do like to feel important in front of everybody.

T: I guess part of what we were talking about is that the feeling of importance has become to some extent external.

H: Yes.

T: One of the theories I'm suggesting is that if your wife chooses to go to her relatives when you stay home by yourself you feel unimportant by yourself and envious.

H: I would say that's great, go have a nice time, you know. It's great. You're going to have a good time. I'll go sailing. But I would say to a certain extent that when she did go I wouldn't say anything. But it would come up. It bothered me.

T: Well, I guess part of it is the sense of lack of initiative on your part. The whole thing doesn't come up with you saying "I'm going sailing this Saturday, going by myself, and I don't want you around." I want you to have fun whatever you're going to do.

W: That doesn't happen though. *(Wife interrupts!)*

T: It does happen though?

W: Yeah. It does happen. *(Wife interrupts again!)*

T: *(to wife)* You'll get a chance.

W: I'm sorry.

H: Yeah. No, she's right again. Because basically I can find things to do if she feels the need to go home.

T: Em hm.

W: And—

H: And the opposite also happens. If I decide to go away for a couple of days, then it works out well.

T: Em hm.

H: She's got the time and she'll take that opportunity to go and see her sister or her parents. I don't think I'm resentful of that part at all. Obviously I've got what I wanted and initiated that . . .

T: Em hm.

H: But I can't handle it the other way around. I don't think.

T: What's your theory about that?

H: I don't know. I just can't stand to see her being pushed around by anybody. I think that's part of it. You're really getting sucked in badly and I can't stand that with anybody. It just disgusts me and I will refuse to believe that she's going to put up with that. I think she's brighter about that now.

T: Part of—

H: . . . realistic . . .

T: Your theory about that is that it was a big issue with you and your family that you handled by cutting them off. I'll forget them. So what you're saying is, Why can't you be more like me?

H: Yup. I guess I am.

Therapist Theories

After listening to the couple for several weeks, the therapist may develop some theories about the difficulty. The therapist may say, "I have a theory that the good opinion of your children is more important than your own closeness. What do you think about my theory?" Another example is, "I believe you have a marriage like one between your father and her mother. What kind of marriage do you think you might have?"

T: The idea of this therapy is not that specific concrete pieces of information come out so much as you disclose your assumptions. You both understand each other a little better. You said you feel closer. You're both willing to listen a little better. That's what it's mainly about. There are no specific answers. I guess the answer to your last question is that the increased knowledge and understanding helps in terms of comparing yourselves to other couples. It also helps in redefining what you want for your marriage.

H: Em hm.

T: A common thing that happens to couples is that they find they are much more functional by making fewer demands on one another for time when previously they thought that that's what ideal marriages are.

H: We don't make great demands for each other as far as time. You know I certainly think that therapy helped an awful lot. I was sort of skeptical to start with, but I certainly see things in a new light. I was disgusted with her relatives with regards to Mary. When I was on this training course, I did a series of tests and this gave me a personality profile. It was amazing, bang on, the way I am when I work.

T: Em hm.

H: You know, stubborn, ambitious, aggressive, so and so forth. I didn't realize the tests I did could be so significant.

T: What were you thinking while your husband was talking?

W: We also looked at that and we said that we thought that it was a very good personality profile for myself as well.

T: Em hm.

W: And we thought, gee there it is you know opposites attract, but we are similar in our envy and stubbornness.

T: What were you thinking?

H: You know we could see that we were very similar and that's what caused the problem.

T: I agree.

H: I don't think—

T: The essence of it is that for a compatible marriage similar traits are more important than different traits. The problem is that you both accept that you are stubborn, aggressive, and jealous—and that's fine. It's only when one of you says that the other one is stubborn, aggressive, and jealous that it becomes a problem.

W: Another line in this test said you must have the last word, you must always have it done your way. There were a lot of qualities in there I thought gee you know I really don't want to have those qualities. We both realize that we not only have it in our professional lives, we have it in our marriage as well. And out when you are working at a job, you know, it's OK . . .

T: Em hm.

W: I think to state your point of view and follow it through is good at work, but at home I think it has to be give and take from both of us. We have to learn to discuss without fighting. I can see one more thing that is causing an awful lot of strain on me in this marriage. Scott's not as concerned about it as I am. At times I guess I get upset at him because he's so nonchalant about it. Like big deal. It's the pregnancy factor.

T: Em hm.

W: That's really getting me depressed. Now I just got sort of a bit of good news that I'm trying to look at very optimistically and hope that something can be done. But still if it finally comes down that no it's just never going to happen, I will be upset.

T: Em hm.

W: I don't think I can cope with that.

T: Why not?

W: Because I want a child so badly. A child of my own.

T: Why do you want a child of your own so badly?

W: I phrased that incorrectly. A child of our own. I realize that I'm sorry that it's my body that won't give me a baby. Maybe our jealousy has interfered.

T: Ah ha.

W: Sorry—

T: Why do you want it? A child of your own so badly?

W: I want to go through nine months of pregnancy. I want to feel everything that you're supposed to feel. I want a baby. I want someone because we both have a lot of love to give to a child. I think, you know, we can, we certainly have got a nice home, and are quite capable of you know really just doing a lot for a child. In everything.

This couple found that therapy led to a significant reduction in arguments. A few years later they were able to have the child they wished.

THERAPIST NONACTIONS (DON'TS)

Feelings

The therapist should suppress the tendency of some spouses to react emotionally by saying they feel angry, hurt, or sad. The expression of these emotions by shouting, arguing, crying, and threatening should be controlled. This does not mean you should be insensitive, but that these feelings and behaviors should not become the focus of therapy or be utilized as resistances to inhibit a spouse from honestly disclosing his or her thoughts. The therapist should focus on patients' cognitive theories of why they reacted in a specific way or why they feel sad or angry.

Mind Reading

The therapist should always remember that the major task is *cognitive* and *self-disclosure.* The therapist should identify and suppress the common tendency of couples in distress to use projection and self-justification such as "My husband thinks I'm useless!" or "Of course, I keep things from my wife since her affair." These remarks are cognitive but *not* self-disclosure. The therapist should ask something like "Why do you think you are married to someone whom you perceive belittles you?" or "What's your theory of why you are married to a woman who had an affair?" The answers, which might be "My family used to belittle me" or "I was afraid to seek revenge," will potentially lead to self-disclosure.

Behavior

The therapist should *not* identify, confront, or comment on the couple's behavior in the sessions with comments such as "I notice you look out the window when your wife is talking" or "You both look as if you are bored with this process." These behaviors, if they are thought to be interfering with the process of cognitive self-disclosure, should be identified only as an interference with the treatment contract. These behaviors *should* be noted and brought to supervision before action is taken.

Interaction

All interruptions should be noted for the content of the self-disclosure is usually crucial for understanding the couple's conflict. However, the therapist should warn the couple that if interruptions continue, the session will be discontinued. The interruptions should also be brought to supervision. The therapist should take *control* and stop arguments, interruptions, and overtalkativeness.

Resistances

You should keep in mind that the couple has explicitly agreed to come to 10 sessions, attempt to answer questions honestly, and participate in cognitive self-disclosure. If both members of the couple say that they do not want to continue, their wishes should be respected after they are reminded of the treatment contract.

If only one spouse does not wish to continue, the reasons should be explored. Phone calls should be accepted only if material disclosed can be revealed to the spouse in the next session. The same applies to individual meetings. Refusal to self-disclose, attend, or respect silence should lead to termination.

SUPERVISION

Supervision of the therapy is done by audiotape and focuses on the therapist behavior. Techniques which overcome resistances are explored and therapists are trained in how to ask cognitive questions. Countertransference reactions of the therapist *reacting* rather than *responding* to a couple *usually* are manifest by the therapist stating that one spouse is causing the therapy to fail.

The audiotape allows observation of standardized questions being asked and to ensure the *do's* and the *don'ts*. Resistances and situations where the couple *react* are discussed to help understand the interactive patterns of marriage and to suggest possible questions for the therapist. Countertransference is identified. Possible reasons for one spouse trying to elicit the therapist's advocacy can be entertained.

CLINICAL EXAMPLES OF THERAPY

In this section several case examples demonstrate what couples reveal about themselves in therapy. I describe the course of therapy over the 10 sessions, using material derived from audiotapes, which is reported verbatim, although it is edited for reasons of confidentiality. My comments about the process should clarify technical points.

Case 1

Sally is a 28-year-old, single, unemployed woman living with her parents. She was referred by her endocrinologist, who felt she had problems with her psychosocial identity.

On initial interview, she appeared younger than her stated age, timid, shy, with marked facial acne. She was almost totally uncommunicative and withdrawn. She demonstrated looseness of association with sexual and hypochondriacal preoccupation. She had a delusional belief that she had venereal disease and hypothyroidism. Her affect was markedly blunted. Her diagnosis was simple schizo-

phrenia in a schizoid personality. She was transferred to
the psychiatric floor where she received Stelazine (10 milligrams four times daily), group psychotherapy, and individual supportive psychotherapy and became more talk-
ative and less withdrawn. An initial family assessment
revealed that her parents wanted her to separate from the
home.

Her past history revealed her first psychiatric assessment
had occurred eight years earlier. She was referred by an
obstetrician who was investigating her for virilism and
endocrine disorder because of withdrawal, shyness, and
increasing isolation. She was preoccupied with mastur-
bation. It was noted by history that her mother was also
a shy, timid person who had been sick most of her life
with hypothyroidism. The father was working away from
home. A diagnosis of schizoid personality with the possibility of a paranoid schizophrenic illness was made. She
was treated with Stelazine and urged to leave home and
work as a lab technician.

Four years later she was seen by a second psychiatrist
complaining of her delusional belief of having venereal
disease. She reported being molested by teenage boys
between the age of 6 and 11 years. She had an idea of
reference that people thought she was soliciting the attention of men. She said her parents were good to her.
A diagnosis of borderline schizophrenia was made and
there was no specific treatment.

Because her placement in a boarding home and sheltered
workshop in a city away from her parents was failing, a
family therapy assessment interview was arranged. The
assessment revealed a marked lack of closeness in her
parents' marriage, and the patient revealed her belief that
if she left home her parents would separate. (A videotape

of this interview is available.) The parents accepted their lack of intimacy as a possible influence on their daughter's current behavior. The following is a synopsis of the self-disclosure of the parents in only five subsequent therapy sessions and their resolution of marital discord.

Mrs. A. revealed her parents lacked closeness and separated when she was 7. Why? Her mother cared for her own sickly mother and shunned men until a late age, eventually inheriting a wealthy farm. The women in her family believed having land was more important than having a man. Mrs. A.'s mother married a man with the second best farm in the area. They argued over the farms and lived separately a few miles apart. Mrs. A. remembers her father's visits as filled with swearing and accusations that her mother was a whore. She vowed that she would never marry and because of her hypothyroidism lived as a recluse on an isolated farm looking after her mother and her farm.

Mr. A. revealed his mother physically abused him as a child. His father ignored these beatings by isolating himself in his religion. Mr. A. escaped from home at age 15 and went to sea. The lack of closeness in his family made him vow to avoid marriage. He lived alone in rooming houses.

While in their forties, both decided to marry for companionship in their old age. She picked him because he didn't swear and he picked her because she was sick and he could look after her. She stayed on their farm to look after her ailing mother and he worked 100 miles away and came home on weekends.

To their surprise, she became pregnant with the patient. It was a difficult pregnancy; the infant was colicky, and they had no one to assist them with mothering or parenting as her mother was senile.

To their further surprise she became pregnant again. He accused her of infidelity because she paid more attention to the relatives on the farm than to him. She denied this. The baby, a boy, died at birth from a cord asphyxiation. Mrs. A. believed that her husband's accusations and medical incompetence caused the death. He believed her infidelity and venereal disease caused the death. They informed the patient of the death of her infant brother. They denied previous self-disclosure of their beliefs to each other or to the patient. The death drove the couple apart and a mutual grudge developed. They both believed they should not have married, should hever have had children, and would have separated after the death of their infant except that they both vowed that they would not separate as their parents had, but stayed together for the sake of the patient.

At this point, the couple and I thought we understood why they had never developed intimacy (five sessions). They decided they would stay together for the companionship they originally wished for, but would explicitly tell their daughter she was no longer necessary to maintain the marriage, although she was welcome in the home.

The patient at follow-up is living on her own, working, socializing, and symptom-free although she remains shy and timid and is on Stelazine (10 milligrams twice daily). (This young woman is still living on her own without further hospitalization seven years later.)

Case 2

A typical family is illustrated by the Smiths (a fictitious name). Mr. and Mrs. Smith presented with their 4 year old, who was encopretic. The Smiths were married 14½ years and had two children, aged 14 and 12 years, and two younger children, who were 4 and 2 years old. They married when Mrs. Smith became pregnant. They were attracted to each other because of their strong dependency needs. During the first three years of marriage, Mr. Smith "ran around" and drank excessively. The couple separated for about three months and then reunited for a reason they identified as "a need for each other." They tried very hard to improve their relationship for the next six years and made attempts to engage in marital therapy. They then decided to start a second family against the second therapist's advice. This is when the two younger children were born in quick succession. As a result of these two pregnancies, finances became a problem; they sold their house because they required a larger one, and Mr. Smith began to change jobs frequently. All the old resentments, anxieties, and anger reemerged and were reinforced. During the year prior to therapy, Mr. Smith had been increasingly depressed and lacked the motivation to sustain the marriage. One more therapist was consulted but "failed" to help, according to the Smiths. Their sexual relationship was poor, and because Mr. Smith acted out in the past, his wife could not trust him.

Mr. Smith was the oldest of four children. He described his father as violent and his mother as hysterical and dependent. Mr. Smith was a constant source of his father's frustration because, like his father, he was an oldest child; his father projected all of his rage and resentment over his own unmet dependency needs on his hapless son, who could never do anything right in his eyes. Mr. Smith was beaten regularly by his father because he was "just there," even if he had done "nothing at all." His paternal grandparents had separated before his father was born; as a result, the father had not developed emotional maturity and was always angry. As Mr. Smith's mother consistently failed to intervene on his behalf during the beatings, he never felt protected by her. She had been emotionally deprived as a child and adolescent; her family had experienced many deaths and losses. Mr. Smith managed to distance himself from his family by working on various farms in the vicinity where he lived. He had always been a loner until he met his wife, who "needed" him.

Mrs. Smith was the oldest of five children; there was a 12-year interval between the second-born and the third-born child. She described her father as strict and punitive, but, at the same time, loving. She always felt closer to her father because her mother was erratic and inconsistent. She rebelled when she reached high school age and lied in order to cover up her social activities.

The preceding history did not emerge at one time. It is the result of the assessment interview plus subsequent interviews during which the therapist asked such "why" questions as:

1. Do you have any idea who was the needy person in your family? Why was that person needy?
2. What opinions do you have about this upbringing? Why did you need to be needed?
3. Why was your father so strict?
4. Do you think your mother's behavior upset him?
5. Why did she have rebellious daughters?

This therapeutic process directed the Smiths to think about their families of origin in order to understand the marital conflict between their parents, the nature of the parenting which they and their siblings had received, and why they chose each other. They began to develop theories that they did not know how to be close and affectionate because they had no earlier models, that emotionally they had given up on each other because there was "such a big vacuum," and that they had demanded "compensation from their own children." The transmission of patterns from one generation to the next was highlighted with gentle humor. "In your opinion, do your families appreciate your efforts to create a living monument to their combined memories?" The response was laughter and "It's dumb, isn't it?"

Mr. and Mrs. Smith made much progress. In their final session, they reported that they felt "married" for the first time. They were able to support each other, negotiate when there were disagreements, communicate constructively, and demonstrate respect for each other's differences. The encopresis in the 4 year old had completely cleared up. The two older children had begun to carry out practical chores, once the heated demands ceased, and they were described as generally helpful to their working parents. The two younger children were better behaved and no longer created chaos in the home. The couple experienced a greater feeling of intimacy and their sexual relationship improved with the decrease in their anxiety.

Case 3

The couple sought a marital assessment six months after their marriage. The couple were professionals in their late twenties. A difference of opinion regarding which should be primary—the husband's career or their relationship—

was the presenting problem. They also had a difference of opinion regarding the wife's wish to have a child and the husband's wish to delay it until their relationship improved. The final presenting problem was an imbalance in expression of affection, with the husband being critical and the wife withdrawing affection when hurt. The couple had many strengths in their relationship including their commitment to the marriage, a good sexual relationship, similar background, and a willingness to talk about the relationship.

The couple accepted that their differences of opinion regarding issues of control and dominance and the subsequent arguments were producing increasing distance and they agreed to participate in Cognitive Family Therapy.

In the first session, the husband disclosed that he had a strict, overbearing father who dominated him through fear, but was isolated both from his wife and from the children. He described a passive but undermining mother, who was emotionally invested in the children. His parents differed markedly in their attitudes toward parenting. The wife disclosed that she had not been close to either parent. She had been involved in considerable acting-out behavior at about the time her father had been involved in an affair. She was forced to keep this a secret from her mother. The therapist focused their attention on answering the following cognitive questions: Why did his mother undermine his father and why was his father so strict? and Why did her father cheat on his wife and why did her mother stay in the relationship?

In the second session, the wife revealed that her mother was a cold, suspicious, and proud woman who had picked a man who had a reputation as a lady's man. She disclosed that her mother's mother had been domineering. She said that her mother had a brother who had had two divorces and had married a very disturbed woman. The husband disclosed that giving his wife what she wanted, in terms of the primacy of their relationship, would be considered a weak and shameful thing in his family. He related this weakness to his father's alcohol abuse. The cognitive questions for the wife in this session were why her father was so dishonest and why her mother was unwilling to face the truth about the relationship; questions for the husband were why his father drank and why his mother was subtly dominating.

In the next session, the wife revealed her desire to get close and have a companion for a husband. This was important to her as she had not seen it in her own parents' marriage or her childhood. The husband reported a need to be needed by a stranger, but not by his wife, again, because if you need a wife you will be seen as weak and effeminate. During this session a shift occurred in which the husband, who had previously seen his alcoholic father as dominating, began to perceive more the isolation and ineffectiveness of his father within the family setting. His wife began to identify her mother's coldness and lack of reality testing, which she thought might have been an explanation for her father's cheating.

In sessions 5, 6, and 7, the wife revealed that her father's father had committed suicide at the death of his wife. Her father had a brother who also had committed suicide and another brother who was divorced. She disclosed that her father was totally cut off from his brothers, but she had no idea what grudge had led to this. She revealed that her mother's father had a reputation for emotional coldness, that her mother's brother had had a divorce, and that the wife of the divorced brother had told her that her grandparents were both cold, unemotional people as well. In these sessions, the husband revealed that his father had also had a brother who was an alcoholic and a weak, ineffectual man dominated by his wife. He also disclosed that his mother had a mother who was a big, dominating woman, who again dominated her husband.

In these sessions the cognitive questions shifted dramatically for the wife to an attempt to understand why the men in her family committed suicide and why the women were so emotionally cold. The husband tried to understand why the men were so helpless in their interpersonal relationships with women and why the women were so tricky and powerful. In this session, the original conflict was identified in terms of the wife's demand that she be put first or the husband might die literally and figuratively. The husband's demand was that she ask directly for companionship and affection rather than being tricky and forcing it out of him by emotional coldness. The clarification of this family issue led to self-disclosure of both the husband and wife of how violent their arguments had been in terms of moderate physical abuse.

In this session the husband explained his views that his wife came from a disturbed marriage in which neither parent had expressed any interest in her, explaining her need for companionship and closeness. He also had not observed closeness in her parents' marriage. He understood that his parents had had a battle for control, although now he had a different and new theory regarding the power balance. The wife revealed that she now understood she had come from a seriously disturbed family and marriage. She was uncertain whether facing this reality helped or hindered her adjustment. She believed that understanding how her husband's family was also seriously distressed provided some relief. The husband disclosed that he felt if he gave his wife the companionship and affection that she demanded he would lose some of his own self-esteem and that her demands would be incessant. The wife disclosed that her husband's insecurity and need for understanding had not previously been apparent to her.

In the ninth session, in a discussion regarding why they wanted to have a child, they revealed that they wanted to have a child in order to give that child the things they had felt deprived of while growing up in their families. The husband wanted to give the child understanding and acceptance. The wife wanted to give the child closeness and companionship. The therapist presented the theory to them that these were the things they wanted from each other and asked the cognitive question "why it was so difficult for them to give to each other what they wanted." The wife disclosed that she was willing to give him what *she* wanted, closeness or companionship, but like her parents she was unwilling to accept that this was not what *he* wanted in terms of his wish for understanding and acceptance. The husband disclosed that he was unwilling to give the closeness and companionship unless he got the understanding he wanted, and that he feared loss of his self-esteem if he gave her what she wanted.

In the tenth session the couple discussed their clinical progress and also gave their subjective opinions about what in therapy had led to improvement. Their arguments had decreased both in severity and frequency. They felt closer to one another and were more able to listen and talk about both their own families and their personal situation. The husband had made professional changes in order to spend more time with his wife, and the wife was spending more time listening to his concerns and insecurities. They both felt that understanding that their parents had not been close and had had a strikingly similar battle for control to what they had experienced, and an increased understanding of why the parents had behaved like this, had a powerful impact on them.

They both felt their needs had been clearly stated and were being understood in terms of the motivation for these needs within their own upbringing and background. The clinical material presented in this case report is typical of the clinical material revealed in the course of Cognitive Family Therapy involving never before discussed family issues of suicide, alcoholism, power conflicts, sexual frigidity, and affairs. The couples' experience of increasing self-disclosure regarding serious psychological difficulty in their parents' interpersonal relationship, and their families as a whole, is typical and provides a greater understanding of the source of marital pathology within their own relationship. A specific theoretical interpretation frequently is neither developed nor apparently important to the couples being treated.

Case 4

This case is presented to provide a description of each of 10 sessions of cognitive self-disclosure. The husband came to see me for depressive symptoms. These symptoms related to frequent arguments in his marriage, indecision regarding his professional career, and unresolved feelings toward his parents, particularly focusing on their overt demands for professional success.

The couple's major problems were arguments reflecting their difficulty in resolving conflict, their poor relationships with their parents on both sides, as well as his relative lack of commitment at this point in time to the relationship. He was actively considering divorce and had greater difficulty than his wife in expressing his thoughts and feelings openly. Strengths in their relationship included their adequate sexual relationship and feelings of self-esteem and identity. The wife perceived their lack of compatibility as being low in terms of their interests and activities, and there was little or no attempt on the part of the couple to present themselves as socially desirable.

His depressive symptoms were significantly improved following the sessions. He demonstrated improved scores on the conflict resolution, cohesion, and autonomy scales of the Waring Intimacy Questionnaire. The couples' total intimacy score increased from 21 to 28 over the 10-week period.

Now let us turn to the description of the process through which cognitive self-disclosure leads to increased closeness. The Cognitive Family Therapy assessment interview revealed that her parents had separated when she was a teenager because her father had had an extramarital affair. Her mother was the youngest girl in her own family, in which marital disharmony focused on her grandfather's alcoholism. Her father was the oldest boy in his own family and had complained of a tricky and dominating mother and an ineffectual father. She believed that her mother withheld affection and sexuality from her father because of his ineffectual professional performance. She assumed that marital maladjustment in her grandparents' marriage was due largely to ineffective, dishonest men.

He disclosed that his mother was tricky and domineering and that his father had married her for social acceptance. He described his mother as sexually and emotionally frigid for a variety of reasons, but primarily because of her moral-religious orientation. His father was a son of a minister who had been professionally successful and married to his career. He believed that the women in his family were extremely powerful. He stated that he found himself in constant conflict because he did not really know whether his wife wished him to be dominant or submissive.

This assessment interview demonstrates a clinical phenomenon common in couples with marital maladjustment. Both spouses perceived their parents' marriages as maladjusted but believed the maladjustment was almost totally caused by one parent's behavior. In this example, the wife was totally cut off from her father by her attitudes regarding his affair, and the husband avoided his mother, believing she was manipulative.

The first session of therapy started with two questions: Why would a man who resented his mother's emotional domination marry a woman whom he perceived to be manipulative like his mother, and why would she pick a man who was indecisive about his career when her father's professional ineffectiveness had been resented?

They both disclosed that they had not recognized these traits about their spouses during courtship. The next question focused on what theories they had to explain why they had worked so hard at not noticing such traits. Both were able to identify that, if they had at the time, they would probably have chosen not to marry. They then focused on why they thought choosing not to marry at that point in their lives would have been unacceptable. She disclosed that she would have lost an opportunity to marry someone who could provide her with status and security, which she craved. He disclosed that he would lose someone who idealized him.

Now we begin to see the process of cognitive self-disclosure. She is beginning to look at her own assumptions regarding her own insecurity and preoccupation with status and is revealing these private thoughts to him for the first time. She also is beginning to look for explanations by evaluating her mother's interpersonal relationship in a new light. He is beginning to disclose his theories about his own vanity, and his father's. The spouses can share their own theories about one another's families of origin from their own more objective experience and observation of their interactions.

In the next few sessions she began to disclose her assumptions about her own insecurity regarding her unhappy home life. Her parents' separation after she entered college had greatly disturbed her. She began to see that her mother was a dominating, unhappy, and complaining woman with whom she was never close. She had always believed this unhappiness and complaining was a reflection of her father's ineffectual, withdrawn behavior, but she was not willing to accept the possibility that her mother was pushing him away. She described herself as serious and competitively successful in school. She disclosed that her loneliness was her primary motive for marriage. Her major difficulty early in the marriage was her conflict between career and motherhood, which was expressed as irritation that she was delaying having children to focus on her husband's career. She began to talk about her career conflicts and developed a theory that her own insecurity had made it difficult for her to identify priorities in her career.

He disclosed that he came from a rigid religious upbringing with pressure to perform academically to receive respect in the family. His father was a successful professional, who he began to see as self-centered for the first time. He viewed his mother as an unhappy, complaining woman who controlled people by making them feel guilty. He had always had a conflict regarding his career between what was expected and what he wanted. He began to talk about this conflict in his family life. He felt that he had to assume duties and responsibilities as husband and father which he resented. He began to acknowledge his fears of interpersonal closeness and of expressing affection or caring toward his wife and to explore an assumption that his vanity, like his father's, made it painful to acknowledge his lack of comfort in personal relationships.

In the course of the next two sessions, their assumptions about their parents' marriages altered drastically as a result of a visit to his parents for the holidays. The visit provoked considerable arguments about each other's behavior. He disclosed that he did not wish to visit his parents but was afraid to reveal this to his mother for fear that she might become psychotic. He did want to see his brother over the holidays to share his perceptions of his parents with him. He did not share this desire with his wife.

She disclosed that she resented that he was not being honest with himself. Her theory of the origin of this resentment was that she also feared her mother-in-law's reaction if she revealed that she did not wish to visit her home. She had difficulty in comprehending his wish to speak with his brother about the family situation and disclosed her envy of this closeness. She said that she was not close with her own brother and did not want to talk with him because he did not perceive his father's adulterous behavior as negatively as she did, and because he had traits similar to their father. She also mentioned for the first time the death of her next youngest brother six years earlier. She began to become more aware that the emotional distance she tried to maintain from her family of origin, and her psychological ignoring of her own father, placed an inordinate amount of responsibility on her husband to be both her husband and family.

He disclosed that he wanted to speak with his brother because he shared a similar perception of his parents. He said that his older brother, who remains single and in the home, is more accepting of their parents' eccentricities. He is not close to this single brother. He disclosed for the first time that it was feasible that the brother living at home might be homosexual. He had never discussed these thoughts with his wife.

She disclosed that, obviously, her father had enjoyed sex, and that this was what led to his affair, for which she could not forgive him. She also perceived her father as a dirty old man who had married a 16-year-old girl, her mother, when he was 32 years of age. Her older brother (who had died) was apparently quite likeable but very irresponsible and inconsistent, and this was a major loss for her, which she had never previously discussed with her husband.

At this point, as the amount of self-disclosure increased, the content was becoming more personal and the spouses were reciprocally sharing ideas about their families they had never discussed before. Theoretical assumptions about the origins of suicide attempts, infidelity, and homosexuality in their families were being shared. At the end of these two sessions, I suggested to both of them that they try to talk to their siblings and get more information about their parents' courtships and their grandparents' marriages. In the seventh and eighth sessions they reported they were getting along much better, talking and listening to one another more frequently, and making more realistic plans for their joint future and his professional plans.

In session 8 she disclosed that she had spoken to her mother at some length and was more aware than she previously had been of her mother's emotional coldness and sexual frigidity, which may have contributed to her father's sexual affairs and physical and verbal abuse toward her mother. She had learned that her mother had also experienced emotional distance and coldness from her own mother. She disclosed that she was still reluctant to talk at length with her father, but she had tried to talk with her brother. She became more aware that a distance from her own family had put an additional burden on her husband. He disclosed that he was more aware of his father's selfishness and vanity contributing to his mother's preoccupation with him as an idealized son. He disclosed his theory that his wife expected him to be reliable and conscientious because of her fear of abandonment. I shared with him my theory that his wife was also looking to him for emotional closeness and support, which she had not received from her mother. He went on to disclose his discomfort at being expected to be caring and close.

They ended this particular session with an attempt at compromise and negotiation regarding his new career plans. He disclosed that he was better able to accept his wife's disappointment and irritation at a real loss in their living style. He disclosed that he had been unprepared to accept her emotional states for what they were because he assumed that, like her mother, she would get even with him in subtle and deceitful ways. She disclosed an awareness of his fears of her feeling states which forced her to behave in a superficially phony way rather than reveal her true feelings. He was developing an increased awareness of his own selfishness and vanity causing his wife to be unhappy and frustrated in the real circumstances of their marriage.

The next to last interview discussed the possibility of incest in his family and, although they both believed the possibilities of incest were not likely, he was able to disclose that his grandmother had accused his mother of such behavior. He assumed that his fears of closeness with his wife might be related to this family secret. She was also more aware that her emotional closeness toward him was promoting the possibility of sexual infidelity in order to replicate the grudge that she held toward her father.

In the last session they reported they felt much closer, were able to listen to one another, and had made new commitments to their relationship and changed their expectations of one another. They discussed what they felt had been helpful to them. They both agreed that they had learned to be better listeners and to accept both the feelings and thoughts of their spouses without denying the reality of these experiences. They both agreed that they had a different cognitive impression of their parents' relationships and the interactions between them which contributed to their own difficulty and could better see how these had influenced their own relationship.

5

Research

Psychotherapy is evaluated by its efficiency, effectiveness, and humaneness. All psychotherapies share features such as providing hope and restoring morale. Psychotherapy attempts to relieve suffering, provide understanding, and do no harm. I will describe a number of research projects designed to evaluate the effectiveness of Cognitive Family Therapy.

EFFICIENCY

Efficiency refers to couples' acceptance of treatment recommendations and completion of therapy sessions as well as early recognition of treatment failure.

Psychotherapy can be effective only if couples and families come for assessment interviews and continue to keep appointments once the therapy has been explained and the sessions commence. One of our first research projects involved the families of psychiatric patients. These patients and families had not requested family assessment or family treatment. Following the assessment interviews, the couples were offered 10 sessions of self-disclosure. The couples attended an astonishing 106 of a possible 110 sessions and there were no dropouts. Experienced family therapists will be surprised, as we were, by this remarkable treatment compliance.

Recently a consecutive series of 24 couples referred for marital assessment was studied. All couples were offered enhancement of marital intimacy and only one couple refused, stating they did not like the idea of cognitive self-disclosure. The compliance rate was again remarkably high. Our clinical experience has been similar.

How does one explain this acceptance of both theory and technique? If the problem which motivated an assessment is defined by the couple as marital discord, the acceptance is almost 100%. If a spouse suffers from anxiety or depression, acceptance is still high. Most parents seem to accept that the quality of their relationship influences the way the family functions and may have a role in initiating or sustaining the symptoms experienced by the family member who is the identified patient. If the identified patient has schizophrenia or a psychosomatic condition, many but certainly not all parents accept that deficient intimacy may precipitate or sustain the problem. Oddly, the theory seems to be more acceptable to our clients than it does to many mental health professionals!

Second, the idea that the interaction between the spouses is the target for intervention seems to reduce feelings of guilt, shame, and blame experienced by many couples. Couples recognize that they have not willfully planned to have a relationship devoid of closeness. Couples are able to see that the observation and experience of their own parents' discord caused them considerable emotional distress. They are able to identify that their emotional distress may play at least some role in the symptomatology of the spouse or the child. The explanation that therapy will involve structured self-disclosure by the spouses or parents alone provides considerable relief to most children. Most children do not wish to attend family sessions. Children are reluctant to disclose their thoughts to their parents. This both reflects the normal barrier between the generations and directly confronts the enmeshment of children in marital conflict described by Minuchin (1974). In fact, the family assessment followed by *only* the parents being in therapy incorporates the basic assumption of structural therapy. Children often are reluctant to reveal observations of their parents which may produce repercussions later in the home. The children also are pleased to see the parents doing something constructive about their difficulties. The majority of couples are accepting of the cognitive disclosures as they provide hope that the negative cycle of personal criticism can be broken. The structure itself relieves anxieties about the unknown expectations of their role in the therapy process. The parents and the therapist may also agree that a child may need specific individual therapy outside of the couple's sessions.

The next question is why so few couples drop out once the therapy sessions have begun. One reason is the brief duration of therapy—only 10 sessions. This raises the hope that the painful discord will be relieved in a short period of time and important decisions regarding separation or divorce can be postponed. Open-ended therapy encourages the notion that therapy will continue until all problems are resolved. The presenting problem may be replaced by discouragement or disappointment with the process as the focus of lengthy therapy.

Another reason for the high compliance with the treatment contract is that self-disclosure of thoughts about relationships is novel and interesting. Couples report that they are proffering information that they never previously discussed. The content often is revealing and challenges the spouses' pigeonholes about spouses and in-laws. Many couples report that the process is fun.

Couples will be concerned about what therapy costs and whether they believe the costs will be worth the potential benefits. Psychotherapy fees vary considerably, but with 10 sessions, a total fee can be calculated and the couple can decide whether the fee is worth the potential benefit to their relationship. I have had couples ask me to show them what they will be getting for their money. I have found the structured nature of self-disclosure easy to demonstrate briefly. I have worked in both a fee-for-service practice as well as a situation where sessions are paid by government insurance, and acceptance was high in both situations. A fixed fee also allows an ease of negotiation in situations where the clients' capacity to pay may be limited. I also find the question of whether their marriage is worth 500 to 1000 dollars a good assessment of priorities and motivation. Obviously there are some couples who are unwilling or unable to pay.

Efficiency also involves speedy identification of whether a psychotherapy is causing more harm than good. I usually advise couples who are contemplating separation or divorce to postpone the decision until the end of the 10 sessions when they will be able to make a more informed decision. Some couples are already separated when they initiate referral. A good sign is if these couples decide to live together during the sessions. If a couple decides to separate during the 10 sessions, it may be that self-disclosure is doing more harm than good. This possibility should be explored with the couple.

Signs that sessions are not going well are varied. One is if each continues to talk about the spouse's motivations rather than self-disclose. This projection must be identified and explained to the couple. Another problem is couples who wish to continue to talk about events or interactions that occur between sessions. This usually suggests a resistance to the process of self-disclosure and/or a wish for more directive advice about problem solving or a more interactional type of psychotherapy. A discussion with the couple about the contract for self-disclosure may be necessary, but also it may be that a different type of counseling is indicated.

The inability to self-disclose usually suggests one of the spouses is becoming depressed. An unwillingness to self-disclose usually suggests a motivational problem. Sessions usually progress from content about the current problem to material earlier in the marriage to material about the parents' marriage. If this process does not occur, it is wise to examine why with the couple. Most couples say that they are talking more at home and the presenting problem is improved or seems less important. The majority of couples who identify early in three or four sessions that the process is not working have been couples with secrets they refuse to reveal, major depressions and alcoholism in one or both spouses, and spouses who refuse to accept responsibility for the marital discord.

When we originally decided to offer 10 sessions, the literature suggested that the average number of outpatient visits for couples was about three sessions! This amazing statistic suggests that the majority of couples do not believe they are getting what they wish from therapy. Most research projects gave a median of about 10 sessions in reports in the literature. Therapists described cases they had seen for one or two years, but these were seldom reported in outcome studies and some therapists suggested length of treatment after about six months often corresponded to poor outcome.

One of our early concerns was whether a large number of couples after completing 10 sessions might want more sessions of cognitive self-disclosure or a different approach. To our surprise, very few couples even suggested that further therapy was needed. The majority of couples reported that the presenting problem was improved, that they were communicating more than previously, and that they had a better understanding of their relationship and their spouse. Some couples suggested more sessions might be helpful and were told to try things on their own for several months and then call back if they still wanted sessions. In a small city feedback about couples going to other therapists, especially where there are few marital therapists, is reasonably good and few couples sought help elsewhere.

Further therapy has been recommended in about 2 out of every 10 cases who completed 10 sessions. However, the therapy recommended is often individual counseling for one or both spouses, sexual counseling, or parental effectiveness training.

In summary, facilitating cognitive self-disclosure is efficient in that most couples assessed accept the treatment contract, complete the sessions, and report satisfaction. Couples doing poorly are usually identified after three or four sessions and alternative approaches are introduced early or accepted after 10 sessions if not satisfied. It has been gratifying to meet these couples later and hear them describe the importance of their sessions to their relationship. Of course there have been some poor outcomes, but there have been few divorces and no expressed dissatisfaction or litigation.

EFFECTIVENESS

Effectiveness refers to whether the therapy is better than no therapy. Comparison to waiting-list controls or ideally to a gold standard of family or marital therapy outcome is the ideal measure of efficacy. Effectiveness is difficult to demonstrate nowadays because withholding active treatment is viewed as unethical; the outcome of couples with discord acting as waiting-list controls is uncertain and there is currently *no* gold standard for family or marital therapy. I will describe the research that has been completed, which unfortunately cannot answer the question definitively about the effectiveness of this approach. However, at least an attempt has been made to objectively evaluate the efficacy of cognitive self-disclosure as a technique to reduce marital discord.

I will describe the treatment of a consecutive series of 24 couples referred for marital assessment. Of the 24 couples, 18 began a course of 10 one-hour sessions of Cognitive Family Therapy.

Previous research including an uncontrolled pilot study, a waiting-list controlled outcome study, and an uncontrolled but objective pretreatment and posttreatment measurement design study suggests that enhancing marital intimacy may be an efficient, effective, and humane treatment approach (Waring & Russell, 1980a). Currently two controlled outcome studies of Cognitive Family Therapy in the treatment of married depressed women and couples in the general population where one or both spouses suffer from nonpsychotic emotional illness are under way. The study of the 24 couples evaluated the efficiency, effectiveness, and humaneness of facilitating cognitive self-disclosure as a marital therapy in privately referred outpatient couples referred to a psychiatrist for assessment of marital maladjustment and/or nonpsychotic emotional illness.

Only two controlled studies have been reported which evaluate the effectiveness of marital therapy in a psychiatric sample. Friedman (1975) reported that marital therapy was effective in the treatment of outpatients with neurotic depression and that the combination of antidepressant drugs and marital therapy was additive. Crowe (1978) reported that directive conjoint marital therapy was superior to a control procedure in neurotic patients. This study focuses on patients with neurosis (nonpsychotic emotional illness).

The 24 couples in this study were *consecutive* referrals to the author from July 1982 to July 1983. They were all private direct referrals to the author from the couple's physician. They represent 25% of the author's outpatient private referrals in this time period. The following four case abstracts represent the range and types of referral problems.

CASE 1

The presenting problem was that the wife had been arrested for shoplifting and the husband had had treatment in the past for a paranoid depressive illness. She had been resentful for years of her husband's overpowering control within the family and more recently of his increased irritability and demandingness related to business reverses and a learning disability in one of their sons. They had another son who had been recently abusing hashish and marijuana, and this had been a concern to both.

They agree that they had been communicating poorly and had slept in separate bedrooms for over a year. She disclosed that her parents had persistent arguments and a lack of communication. He described his father as being somewhat boring and pedantic. She revealed that the major factor precipitating their referral was a close relationship with an older male which she denied was an affair, but which he suspected had been. She revealed that one of the major events in their history was his accepting her sexual activity prior to the marriage and their continued sexual difficulties after the marriage. With the birth of their first child, she became chronically depressed and had had previous psychiatric counseling. Previous marital counseling was unsuccessful.

CASE 2

They both stated that their difficulties had begun about five years earlier at the time that she had treatment for cervical cancer. She felt that he was distant and unavailable for support at that time. He said that he fell out of love with her because she did not seem to be looking after herself and had gained weight.

She feels that she has had to placate him in order to maintain the relationship. She describes this as a lifelong pattern of walking on eggshells or not making waves for fear that the relationship will end. He was married previously and after a couple of years of marriage his wife left him for someone else. They revealed that they had sexual difficulties, with him being overactive and her underactive, from the beginning of their marriage. He described his parents' relationship as not very close. She was adopted as a child, but her adoptive parents split up when she was 7 years old. He refused further therapy at the time, but she was willing to come in on her own to understand herself better.

CASE 3

The presenting problem was ongoing arguments regarding the parenting of their oldest child. She believed that he did not respect her ideas and capacity as a mother. Both agreed that they had not told the daughter that the daughter is the child in their family and that their relationship comes first.

They have been married for nine years and have one child from his previous marriage, a 15-year-old daughter. His first wife was an alcoholic and attempted suicide. He felt guilty about her illness and spent considerable time trying to rescue her. The wife stated that she had a number of relationships with men whom she had picked from the onset because they would not reciprocate her affection. She attributed this to her own insecurity and lack of self-esteem. His parents' marriage was described as constant bickering and arguing, but they are still together. She describes her parents' marriage as being of two people with totally different backgrounds who divorced when she was 20 years of age.

CASE 4

The presenting problem was that he had had a brief affair. The couple said that earlier in their marriage their sexual relationship had been satisfactory, but lately she feels that he is going through the motions without caring. He feels that she is avoiding intercourse. She has had symptoms of clinical depression. She recognizes that she has been depressed for some time because of his lack of caring about her being pregnant, the illnesses of her parents, which have disturbed her, and his preoccupation with his career. She describes her parents as being very close and very affectionate with one another. He describes his parents as compatible, but leading largely separate lives. There was some question about his commitment to the ongoing relationship and they considered a separation.

All 24 couples were seen for a one-hour clinical assessment interview using the approach described in Chapter 3. At the end of this one-hour interview, all couples were offered 10 one-hour sessions of cognitive self-disclosure. The theoretical basis for the therapy was explained to all couples. The specifics of the technique were also explained.

At this time, all couples were asked to complete three self-report questionnaires: the Waring Intimacy Questionnaire (Waring, 1984), the Locke–Wallace Marital Adjustment Scale (Locke & Wallace, 1959), and the General Health Questionnaire (Goldberg, 1972). Details of these questionnaires are presented below with each having adequate reliability and validity. At the end of 10 sessions, the couples were again asked to complete the same questionnaires and an attempt was made to contact all couples at six-month follow-up through questionnaires which were mailed to them.

The therapist and the couples completed a 5-point Likert scale for improvement, unchanged, or worse at the end of the 10-week sessions. An independent research assistant abstracted all 24 cases and made an independent judgment on outcome. The independent research assistant also used the case notes to make an assessment on a 5-point scale on the honesty, interpersonal curiosity, and motivation of the couples prior to treatment.

The Waring Intimacy Questionnaire (WIQ) is a 90-item true–false inventory developed on the basis of principles of personality scale construction utilizing a sequential strategy developed by Jackson (1970). The total intimacy score has been shown to be positively correlated with marital adjustment ($r = .48$, $p < .01$) and valid with regard to perceived intimacy as measured by the Personal Assessment of Intimacy in Relationships (PAIR), developed by Schaefer and Olson (1981) ($r = .77$).

In addition to a total intimacy score, the WIQ offers a qualitative assessment of intimacy along eight dimensions which were described in Chapter 2:

1. *Conflict resolution*—the ease with which differences of opinion are resolved.
2. *Affection*—the degree to which feelings of emotional closeness are expressed by the couple.
3. *Cohesion*—a feeling of commitment to the marriage.
4. *Sexuality*—the degree to which sexual needs are communicated and fulfilled by the marriage.
5. *Identity*—the couple's level of self-confidence and self-esteem.

6. *Compatibility*—the degree to which the couple is able to work and play together comfortably.
7. *Autonomy*—the success with which the couple gains independence from their families of origin and their offspring.
8. *Expressiveness*—the degree to which thoughts, beliefs, attitudes, and feelings are shared within the marriage.

Test–retest reliability of the WIQ ranges from .73 to .90 for the eight subscales, with reliability of .89 for the total intimacy score. The internal consistency of the WIQ, as measured by the Kuder–Richardson 20 statistic, ranges from .52 to .87, with .81 for total intimacy, all within acceptable ranges of consistency for this statistic. A social desirability score (range 0 to 10) is also computed, and this is subtracted from the preliminary intimacy score to yield the final total intimacy score. With the use of the social desirability score, some of the response style bias is removed.

The Locke–Wallace Marital Adjustment Scale is a 16–item self-report questionnaire which assesses marital interaction and marital function; it has been used in marital research since 1959 with established reliability and validity (Locke & Wallace, 1959). The scale has been shown to have high reliability (.90), computed by the split-half technique and corrected by the Spearman–Brown formula. Thus the Locke–Wallace Marital Adjustment Scale has high reliability. In their study of 236 couples, the mean adjustment score for the well-adjusted group (judged to be exceptionally well adjusted in marriage by friends who knew them well) was 135.9, whereas the mean score for the maladjusted group (clients of the American Institute of Family Relations and subjects who were known to be maladjusted in marriage) was only 71.7. This difference was very significant, for the critical ratio was 17.5. Only 17% of the maladjusted group achieved adjustment scores of 100 or higher, whereas 96% of the well-adjusted group achieved scores of 100 or more. These figures indicate that this test clearly differentiates between persons who are well adjusted and those who are maladjusted in marriage. Therefore, the test has validity, since it seems to measure what it purports to measure: marital adjustment.

The final questionnarie, the General Health Questionnaire (GHQ28), is a 28-item self-report questionnaire for the detection of nonpsychotic emotional illness (Goldberg, 1972). It offers a qualitative and quantitative estimate of the degree of psychiatric disturbance in an individual. Four subscales have been identified: somatics, anxiety, social dysfunction, and depression. The results obtained on these four scales have been shown to be positively correlated with psychiatrists' ratings (r = .51 to .76). In addition, the total severity score from the GHQ28 correlates well (r = .76) with psychiatrists' ratings of severity. The scale version of the GHQ is intended for use in general population surveys when more information than that provided by a single severity score is required. In the GHQ28, a cutoff score of between 4 and 5 points has been shown to be both sensitive (88% and 78% of cases were correctly identified in psychiatric interview) and specific (72% and 84% of noncases correctly identified).

Previous reviews of marital therapy outcome research suggest that behavioral approaches and structured approaches focusing on direct communication between spouses are effective, but none of these studies evaluate psychiatric referrals (Gurman, 1973; Jacobson, 1978). Gurman and Kniskern (1975) suggest that there is somewhat less persuasive evidence of the power of these methods with severely distressed couples or with couples with one (or two) severely disturbed individuals.

Psychotherapy outcome research, which measures effectiveness, is clearly strengthened by random assignment to matched control groups. This was omitted in this study for the following reasons:

1. A no-treatment control group would be unethical in the circumstances of private direct referrals for assessment and therapy.
2. Our previous pilot study using waiting-list control groups demonstrated that with marital and family therapy, these couples do not wait and all of our couples on the waiting list in our previous trial obtained help from other sources while they were on the waiting list, supporting Gurman and Kniskern's point that they were not truly untreated (1975). There is also suggestive evidence that there is *no* spontaneous recovery for couples awaiting marital therapy (Johnson, 1984).
3. In order to have a comparative matched control group for this study, another psychiatrist who received 24 outpatient marital assessment referrals in a year would be necessary. There were no such psychiatrists in the London area. Finally, if such a psychiatrist existed, he or she would have to be willing to compare a specific therapy and his or her therapeutic skills in a consecutive series of referrals, and this might be difficult to obtain.

Thus without such a matched control group with careful control of therapist and therapy variables, definitive statements about effectiveness of Cognitive Family Therapy cannot be made. However, the use of a consecutive series controls for selection bias on the basis of client characteristics or expectations. All couples were offered the same therapy independent of these factors.

The results again suggested that this therapeutic approach was efficient and humane. Of the 24 cases referred, 6 couples did not proceed with the treatment contract of 10 one-hour per week sessions of Cognitive Family Therapy at the end of the referral session. Only *one* couple *refused* to participate in the therapy because they did not wish to disclose their private thoughts, ideas, and feelings to one another in the treatment session.

The decision in the remaining five couples was a mutual decision of couple and therapy because:

1. One couple was unable to attend sessions within the time frame offered and was referred to a marital counseling service.
2. One husband refused to participate in therapy and his wife received outpatient psychotherapy individually.
3. One couple who agreed to participate in the trial did not follow up and keep the sessions, because the husband had taken an overdose in order to stop his wife from separating and the overdose produced the desired reunion.
4. One husband and wife had already separated and decided that they did not want the joint sessions in collaboration with the author.
5. One husband was seeing another woman and was not prepared to give her up at this time.

No divorces occurred in the entire sample of 24 couples. Only one couple refused to accept therapy and only one couple dropped out of therapy.

The results with the 18 couples who initiated the 10 one-hour sessions of cognitive self-disclosure were as follows:

1. Using the subjective therapist rating, patients' ratings, and independent assessors' ratings, 12 of the 18, or 67%, were improved at 10-week follow-up.
2. These couples attended and participated in 103 out of a total of a possible 120 sessions, suggesting high compliance.
3. Three couples had improved so dramatically after five, five, and three sessions that with the concurrence of the therapist, they stopped the therapy at that time.

Four couples were rated as being unchanged, although in this group one couple was rated as improved by themselves but as unimproved by the therapist. The first couple of this four attended six sessions, but the husband was out of the country so frequently on business that they dropped out of the therapy. The second couple dropped out of therapy after four sessions without any previous discussion or reason being obvious. The third couple completed the 10 sessions and rated themselves as slightly improved, although the therapist's rating was that there had been little improvement in their relationship. The fourth couple stopped after five sessions because the depression of one of the spouses necessitated specific medication and withdrawal from the trial.

Two couples were evaluated as being worse at the end of the trial. For the first, the therapy stopped after four sessions in order that both spouses could receive individual therapy for treatment of depression. The second couple was stopped again after four sessions as individual sessions for both spouses were recommended. Both of the couples who were considered to be worse had had previous unsuccessful therapy and had significant major affective disorder. Remarkably none of these couples has divorced at six-month follow-up.

The results also suggest that the therapy was effective. Table 5 gives the objective independent ratings of the research assistant rated on a 5-point Likert scale. Reliability and validity of these ratings on the Likert scale were not obtained, thus no statistics are done on these data. It is clear that the good outcome group was objectively rated as having good motivation, more honesty, and more psychological mindedness and interpersonal curiosity than both the poor outcome and no-therapy groups. This is in keeping with much of the psychotherapy outcome research, which suggests that client characteristics are an important source of variance in the outcome of psychotherapy separate from therapist and therapy variables.

Table 6 gives the results of the objective measures of outcome on the three self-report questionnaires. Obviously not all couples could be persuaded to complete the questionnaires at the 10-week or six-month follow-up and often the questionnaires were returned incomplete and thus not suitable for analysis. Clearly as well there is a tendency for the nine couples on which complete data were gathered

Table 5

Ratings of Motivation, Honesty, Psychological Mindedness

Good Outcome (12)	Poor Outcome (6)	No Therapy (6)
9.5	5.8	5.3

n = 24 couples

Table 6
Test Results at 10-Week Follow-Up

Test	Pretherapy	Posttherapy	Significance
Wife's intimacy	16.6	23.1	$p<.04$
Wife's GHQ	14.6	7.6	$p<.005$
Wife's LWMA	73.0	102.3	$p<.02$
Husband's intimacy	20.7	21.8	$p<.65$, n.s.
Husband's GHQ	8.1	1.6	$p<.02$
Husband's LWMA	84.4	101.2	$p<.07$, n.s.

$n = 9$ couples

to be from the better outcome group, but there are several couples from the poor outcome group included. There is a significant reduction in the symptoms of nonpsychotic emotional illness in both husbands and wives. The wife's perceived level of intimacy significantly increased, as did the husband's, but it was not a statistically significant level. The wife's perception of marital adjustment significantly improved and the husband's also improved, but not quite to statistical significance. Table 7 gives the six-month follow-up.

Obviously no definitive conclusions can be reached regarding the effectiveness of Cognitive Family Therapy as a treatment for outpatient marital adjustment and/or nonpsychotic emotional illness in one or both spouses because of the lack of a control group in this particular study. When one compares this study with the existing uncontrolled outcome research on marital therapy, it compares favorably. Beck's review of research findings on the outcome of marital counseling reported on eight published

Table 7
Test Results at Six-Month Follow-Up

Test	Pretherapy	Posttherapy	Significance
Wife's intimacy	14.25	19.75	$p<.35$, n.s.
Wife's GHQ	14.50	2.75	$p<.09$
Wife's LWMA	62.00	82.00	$p<.35$, n.s.
Husband's intimacy	18.25	21.50	$p<.28$, n.s.
Husband's GHQ	5.50	3.75	$p<.37$, n.s.
Husband's LWMA	88.00	99.75	$p<.50$, n.s.

$n = 4$ couples

studies utilizing global ratings on at least 10 cases (Beck, 1966). Improvement ratings ranged from 29% to 92% with a general concentration following in a narrow range from 65% to 70%. This figure is similar to that reported by Gurman (1973), which covered all marital treatment outcome studies reported in journals in the period from 1950 to 1972. His pooled rate of improvement was 61% in the 15 studies that he located which reported global ratings. Beck (1970) reports that only 49% of cases reported by counselors improved in a large follow-up study. She concluded that couples whose core problem involved their marital relationship were relatively difficult to help.

Thus one can only conclude that in this uncontrolled outcome trial, the results are not so poor as to prohibit future controlled trials of this approach. Others have undertaken to review the outcome literature, but as Olson (1970) stressed, the meager research literature in the field on marital counseling has many methodological weaknesses, some of which are highlighted in this study. Unfortunately, even in the outcome studies which involved control groups, the researchers tend to evaluate either communications training procedures or behavior modification approaches and often the patient samples are not typical of couples referred to psychiatrists.

Jacobson's (1978) as well as Gurman and Kniskern's (1975) more recent review also suggest that the two approaches to marital therapy which emerge from the literature as the most promising are the behavioral and conjugal relationship enhancement approaches. However, Jacobson's review suggests that the marital therapies which are brief, time-limited, and relatively structured are to be recommended on the basis of current research.

While the effectiveness of this therapy must await the results of several current control outcome trials, this study does suggest that Cognitive Family Therapy is a relatively efficient and humane type of outpatient marital counseling where one or both spouses suffer from nonpsychotic emotional illness. This is supported by significant reduction in symptoms of nonpsychotic emotional illness in the group with a good outcome and the fact that the unchanged or worse group consisted predominantly of couples where one or both spouses suffered from primary affective disorder.

The third conclusion is that the methodology employed in this trial can be useful to therapists for practice audit. The self-report questionnaires when combined with the subjective therapist, patient, and independent assessor's judgment do provide useful information on the efficiency of psychotherapy, although the research design without matched controls is unsuitable for outcome research which hopes to make comments on effectiveness. The fourth conclusion is that comparison studies with other therapies and other therapists are now feasible using this methodology. The absence of literature regarding such cases referred to psychiatrists suggests that such research is both timely and needed.

The study also confirms several recent reports which suggest that where one or both spouses are suffering from a major affective disorder, marital therapy may be contraindicated (Merikangas, 1984; Ruestow et al., 1978).

In summary, the study suggests that for outpatient couples directly referred to psychiatrists for marital maladjustment, and where one or both spouses suffers from nonpsychotic emotional illness, and where the couple is motivated, honest, and psychologically minded, cognitive self-disclosure appears to be an efficient and humane form of therapy which merits further investigation as to its effectiveness in a controlled research design.

Finally, those readers who believe that I might be biased in presenting only research that supports the effectiveness of my own approach will be surprised with what follows. I do not believe I have read a book on marital or family therapy where the author presents data that demonstrate his or her approach is ineffective or even contraindicated in a specific group of clients!

A recent project was an attempt to replicate a study by Friedman (1975) which demonstrated that the combination of antidepressant medication and outpatient marital therapy was more effective than either alone in a sample of patients with dysthymic or neurotic depression. Our original design replicated Friedman's in that it contained a placebo versus active medication, and placebo marital therapy versus active marital therapy in various combinations.

David Patton and I showed that in depressive hospitalized women with both major depressive disorders and dysthymic disorders, a deficiency in the perceived quality of marital intimacy was highly correlated with the level of depressive symptomatology (Patton & Waring, 1984). Thus we postulated that a specific marital therapy which sought to increase the level of intimacy through self-disclosure might be particularly appropriate for this group of patients.

For these reasons, Friedman's (1975) research design was replicated. However, our sample focused only on women with unipolar, major affective disorder as defined by the Research Diagnostic Criteria and *DSM-III* (Spitzer et al., 1978). Since evidence suggested that antidepressants are an effective treatment for major affective disorders, we decided to reassess Friedman's major findings and study whether or not a specific marital therapy—cognitive self-disclosure—would have an additive effect in combination with the antidepressant doxepin. The study predicted that the combination of an antidepressant and a marital therapy specifically designed to enhance marital intimacy would be similar to two control treatments.

The sample consisted of 27 female married patients between the ages of 18 and 60 who were diagnosed by their physicians as having major affective disorder according to *DSM-III* criteria and were subsequently referred to the study. Two psychiatrists reached a consensus diagnosis of major affective disorder according to the Research Diagnostic Criteria (RDC) (Spitzer et al., 1978). These patients also demonstrated symptoms of depression on the General Health Questionnaire (GHQ) (Goldberg, 1972) and Beck Depression Inventory (BDI) (Beck et al., 1961). All patients were hospitalized at the onset of the study and were not selected on the basis of complaints of marital maladjustment. Informed consent was given by the patients and spouses before participating in the clinical treatment.

Patients were randomly assigned to one of two control groups or to the study group; that is, they received doxepin (Sinequan) and one of two control supportive psychotherapies or they received doxepin and cognitive self-disclosure. The first control group consisted of both husband and wife participating in ten 20-minute sessions with a psychiatrist, one session per week. No specific marital therapy was offered. The second control group involved the woman alone seeing a psychiatrist for ten 20-minute sessions over a 10-week period, and again no specific marital therapy was offered. The patients in the treatment group received 10 one-hour sessions of cognitive self-disclosure over 10 weeks.

All patients received doxepin at a variable dosage between 50 and 250 milligrams daily, adjusted according to therapeutic effects and side effects.

Patients were evaluated by test scores on the self-report BDI (Beck et al., 1961) and the Hamilton Rating Scale for Depression (HAM–D) (Hamilton, 1960). The HAM–D is a structured interview and was conducted by a research assistant who was blind to the patient's treatment group membership. Measurements on the GHQ and Hamilton Rating Scale for Anxiety (HAM–A) (Hamilton, 1959) were obtained on admission and again after 10 weeks. Differences between the pretreatment and posttreatment measures and between groups were assessed by dependent t-tests and one-way analyses of variance (ANOVA), respectively, with the probability of type I errors set at .05.

Fourteen patients failed to complete the 10-week trials and six-month follow-up. Eight of the 14 who dropped out were in the self-disclosure group while 6 of the 14 were in the control group.

According to dependent t-tests, all 13 patients receiving doxepin who completed the trial demonstrated significant improvements in depressive symptoms on the HAM–D (t = 7.07, p < .05), the HAM–A (t = 4.42, p < .05), the BDI (t = 2.56, p < .05), and the GHQ (t = 3.63, p < .05). No significant differences are found between improvement scores in the control and treatment conditions except on the BDI, where there was significantly *less* improvement in the self-disclosure group (Table 8). Supportive care without spouse involvement demonstrated the greatest improvement. Although not statistically significant on all measures, the results were consistently in the opposite direction of the study hypothesis. These findings indicated that the combination of self-disclosure and antidepressants in the treatment of married women with major affective disorder was not superior to the two control conditions.

The results were also supported by a one-way ANOVA. The BDI showed a significant difference among the means (F < 1.0), with no significant improvement in the self-disclosure group.

Fourteen patients failed to complete the 10-week trial and six-month follow-up. Four patients were readmitted to the hospital within 10 weeks and withdrawn from the trial because of high suicide risk. Two patients in the control groups dropped out of the trial at about three weeks because of symptomatic improvement and no wish to continue the trial. One patient dropped out because of drug side effects. Six patients dropped out of the trial for unknown reasons, mostly within the first three weeks of the trial. Three couples separated during the trial, two of

Table 8
Comparison of Improvement in CFT and Supportive
Therapy Groups

Scale	CFT Group	Supportive Care with Spouse	Supportive Care without Spouse	F
BDI	19.6	22.8	24.5	5.01*
	19.6	4.3	2.5	
HAM-D	24.0	23.5	21.5	0.17
	8.7	7.8	2.0	
HAM-A	19.0	22.5	17.0	0.21
	8.0	7.5	1.5	
GHQ	21.0	21.0	18.5	1.45
	14.8	4.8	0.0	

Note: Upper numbers are initial scores; lower numbers are scores at 10-week assessment.

$*p < .05$

whom were in the self-disclosure group. Eight of the 14 who dropped out were in the self-disclosure group, and six were in the control group.

When the couples who received self-disclosure were compared to those receiving supportive care at 10 weeks, there was significantly greater improvement in the *supportive* care group on the BDI. Since this finding and the other nonsignificant results were in the opposite direction to the hypothesis, the trial was discontinued for ethical reasons.

In summary, although the numbers were extremely small, the 13 patients who completed the 10-week trial demonstrated significant improvement in depressive symptoms while taking doxepin. However, those who also received self-disclosure demonstrated *less* improvement than those in the control conditions. Since the dropout rate and the rate of marital separation were higher in the self-disclosure group, the trial was discontinued.

This study demonstrated the effectiveness of antidepressant medication combined with three types of psychotherapy in the treatment of major affective disorder over a 10-week period. However, the combination of doxepin and cognitive self-disclosure was not superior to supportive psychotherapy given to the couple together or the patient alone. The six marital therapists received specific training and continuous supervision during the clinical trial. The results suggest that this therapy is not indicated in combination with antidepressants during the symptomatic phase of major affective disorder.

In fact, the tentative conclusions that antidepressants alone or in combination with supportive therapy are better than antidepressants with a specific marital intervention in major affective disorders finds support in previous reports by Merikangas (1984) and Ruestow et al. (1978). Friedman's study (1975) suggests that in the dysthymic depressions antidepressants plus marital therapy may be additive, but our results suggest that in major unipolar depressions in women the combination of antidepressants plus marital therapy may not be indicated. Our current study on dysthymic married women has shown a trend for the effectiveness of the self-disclosure approach.

Our study suggests that when married women with unipolar affective disorders present problems with their marriage, the initial treatment phase should involve antidepressants plus supportive care. Only after an adequate trial of medication should the possibility of marital therapy be explored with those couples who attribute depression to marital dysfunction. The results also suggest that couples referred for marital therapy should be screened for major depression.

CONCLUSION

The research on Cognitive Family Therapy to date suggests that it is an efficient and humane approach. Compared to most marital and family therapy approaches which have *not* been subjected to carefully controlled outcome trials, it would appear to be equally effective. The effectiveness would appear to be most obvious in couples who present with relationship difficulties and it clearly reduces symptoms of anxiety and mild depression in spouses while increasing their intimacy. Cognitive Family Therapy is definitely not indicated where one or both spouses have a severe depression.

6

Summary and Conclusions

More than 10 years have passed since my study of marital intimacy began. I have described the development of a theory of family dysfunction and the effort to define intimacy which led to the practice of facilitating cognitive self-disclosure. The first five chapters reflect the process that led to the therapy.

During the past 10 years, there has been considerable progress in family and marital assessment and therapy. I have read material that I was unaware of 10 years ago or that was not available until recently. My publications have been reviewed, criticized, and commented on by colleagues and students. I next attempt to integrate my own work with these recent developments.

I begin by returning to the original theory, which hypothesized that marital intimacy was crucial to normal family functioning. Has the experience with the therapy modified the ideas that stimulated its development? What light has therapy shed on our concepts of marital adjustment, marital discord, and health and dysfunctional family environments?

THEORETICAL DEVELOPMENTS

When my research began, three theoretical approaches were utilized by marital and family therapists: psychoanalytic, behavioral, and systems. The psychoanalytic perspective attempts to understand marital discord and family difficulties by understanding the unconscious motives and conflicts of individuals as they present in close relationships. The behavioral approach attempts to understand couples and families by analyzing the consequences of various behaviors which may lead to repetitive sequences. The systems approach understands the couple and family as a whole and attempts to clarify the relationship of the whole to the parts and vice versa.

There are strengths and weaknesses to each of these theories. Psychoanalysis involves a pessimistic view of human nature and necessitates complex and lengthy techniques to make the unconscious material conscious. On the positive side, it helps explain why some spouses select obviously incompatible mates and why relationships with obvious discord are often maintained. Behavioral approaches can lead to specific interventions which, if honestly attempted, will result in improvement but fail to explain why many couples and families refuse to implement even obvious suggestions. Systems theory suggests that families will resist change unless confronted or tricked, but these types of interventions often lead couples and families to drop out of therapy.

However, my greatest reservation was that each of these theories was developed from observations that had little to do with couples and families: hysterical Viennese women, rats, and biological systems such as cells. I hoped to develop a theory that was related primarily to our knowledge about marriage and families. I employed Eric Erikson's notion that the major psychosocial task of young adulthood was the development of intimacy (Erikson, 1950). Although this theory, which was described in Chapter 2, is clearly more central to the beginning marriage and families, it is not without serious limitations.

First, it is clear that the majority of couples do not consciously choose to marry to develop closeness. Most couples report that they marry because they are in love, because they want security, to enjoy sex or start a family, to enjoy companionship, or to escape loneliness or unpleasant situations. While we can describe the quality of these relationships in terms of intimacy, this is not a prime conscious motive. We could suggest an unconscious wish or need for intimacy, but this is not without its own set of problems. An unconscious intimacy motive would be one among many presumed needs including sexual, aggressive, and dependence dynamics. We would have to invent a developmental theory of why the intimacy motive is primary while it is obvious that not everyone wishes or values close heterosexual relationships.

Second, intimacy is not the only interpersonal construct that defines couples. The relationship of intimacy to power and boundary would need to be clarified. Problems with intimacy are not the only issues raised by couples in distress. It is also obvious that couples do not decide to separate only on the basis of psychological distress, nor is deficient intimacy the only distressing behavior one can find in a family.

Finally, one is left with the same dilemma in explaining the importance of self-disclosure. Self-disclosure is only one aspect of communication and can hardly be expected to explain all marital discord.

Fortunately, the personal construct theory of Kelly provides an approach which allows us to integrate both intimacy and self-disclosure in understanding marriage and the family (Kelly, 1955). Kelly suggests that each person acts like a scientist who develops conscious personal constructs in an attempt to anticipate relationships. The theory suggests that these cognitive schemas are developed through attempts at understanding the relationships we observe and experience growing up. These personal constructs about our parents' marriages have been shown to transfer from our parents' marriages to our own marriages.

This theory suggests that our marriages are like experiments in which we pigeonhole significant others, particularly our spouses, and look for evidence to support our beliefs. A man may have developed the personal construct that women cannot be trusted through attempts to understand his parents' persistent arguments which he observed and experienced. He will look for evidence in his wife's behavior in order to confirm his belief system. He will ignore behaviors that are discrepant from his idea. He may even behave in a way that might provoke untrustworthy behavior. Kelly suggested that a therapist should help both spouses experience one another as discrepant from their "cognitive schema." One method of accomplishing this is to help spouses disclose these "personal constructs" and explore how they were developed in observation and experience of personal relationships in the family.

Segraves (1982) outlines a theoretical integration of differing approaches to the treatment of marital discord which suggests a cognitive approach. Segraves develops Kelly's model and suggests that 1) faulty cognitive schemas of close relationships with the opposite sex are of primary importance in the genesis and maintenance of marital discord; 2) spouses tend to behave toward spouses in such a way as to invite behaviors that are congruent with personal constructs; and 3) maladaptive interactional patterns maintain individual psychopathology in spouses.

These personal constructs develop through attempts to understand the discord which is observed and experienced in the parents' marriage. Couples with marital discord or family dysfunction will note that distress in their parents' marriage caused the observer emotional distress in childhood. But it is clear that our personal constructs about individuals are more fully developed than our constructs about relationships. Rather than understanding one's parents' discord as a couple problem, these spouses understand the distress in constructs of one of the parents being responsible for the maladjustment. For example, a father's drinking or a mother's bossiness may be offered as an explanation of the discord. When asked why the father drank or why the mother was bossy, the offspring will usually say they never thought about it. But the couple will report that they looked for a spouse who did not drink or was not bossy.

These offspring will ignore thinking about the interaction between father's drinking or mother's bossiness. They will often discover in therapy that they behave toward their spouse in a way which will invite behaviors congruent with their personal constructs. The failure of the offspring to understand why power in relationships can be organized in a variety of ways limits their own ability to resolve power issues in their marriage. In summary, in an attempt to understand the unbalanced power dysfunction, an individual may attribute to a spouse a characteristic of a parent thought to be responsible for marital discord which caused the individual psychological suffering.

A cognitive view of psychotherapy is exerting a major influence on therapeutic practice. Examples include Beck's use of cognitive restructuring to alter negative self-concept in depression and Meichenbaum's cognitive behavior therapy (Beck, 1967; Meichenbaum, 1977). Greenberg and Safran (1984) suggest that cognition and affect operate as two independent systems in human experience. Rachman (1984) suggests that if the problem lies in the cognitive system, the therapeutic interventions should focus on the personal constructs although feelings may vary accordingly. Does the problem of failure to develop, maintain, or sustain intimacy in marriage reside in the cognitive domain?

Bowlby (1985) recently wrote about the influence of childhood on cognitive development. He suggests that disturbances in cognitive development are created in three ways: 1) knowledge that the parents wish to deny the child; 2) knowledge that the couple wish to prevent the child from disclosing; and 3) information that the child does not wish to think about. Bowlby uses the dramatic example of children who have witnessed a parent's suicide attempt. Children may be told that they have not seen what they thought they had observed. Knowledge of why the attempt occurred will be denied the child, the child may be prevented from disclosing his thoughts about the incident and the child may learn to keep his thoughts to himself or even doubt his perception of reality.

There are many other types of events, observations, or knowledge which are consciously withheld from children. The couple will often have knowledge of the circumstances of a child's conception which must influence parents' attitudes toward a child. The quality of the relationship at the time of conception may be secure and loving or a casual sexual liaison. Surely a child born into these very different relationships could not be expected to receive the same quality of mothering or to observe and experience the same quality of marital intimacy. This knowledge, which is withheld from the child, often becomes the focus of the family's dysfunction. How often do family therapists see the child who thinks she does not belong (the adopted child who has never been told) or the child who feels responsible for the parents' discord (the child who was responsible for a forced marriage)? If the couple fail to disclose the basis for attitudes, how can accurate personal constructs and interpersonal curiosity develop? If the couple insist that a child has not observed or experienced circumstances such as physical abuse, sexual abuse, or suicide attempts, how can reality testing through self-disclosure develop?

Second, a child attempts to understand observations and experiences with the quality of his parents' intimacy. The child may observe a couple demonstrating indifference, hostility, cruelty, and dishonesty, but may not be allowed to ask why the couple do not seem to like one another. The child may be told that the couple love each other but witness the opposite or at least fluctuations.

Finally, children may learn to keep their thoughts to themselves for fear of consequences or suppress the thoughts because they are too painful.

Kelly's personal construct theory provides a broader model for understanding the importance of self-disclosure in the development of intimate relationships (Kelly, 1955). The theory suggests that conscious personal constructs developed through the observation and experience of deficiencies of intimacy in the parents' marriage will interfere with the development of close relationships if not disclosed.

While intimacy has found a theory, how has the practice of self-disclosure therapy and the research it has stimulated modified the original idea that deficiencies in the quality and quantity of marital intimacy define dysfunctional families?

The major modification would be that if self-disclosure is considered one type of communication, the use of structured self-disclosure as a therapy may be useful independent of the concept of intimacy. Poor communication is characteristic of marital maladjustment. Communication involves clear messages, attentive listening, congruence between content and process, and self-disclosure, to name a few aspects (Noller, 1984). Improved self-disclosure might be therapeutic independent of whether intimacy changes. The theoretical and clinical importance of cognitive self-disclosure has been supported by the many couples who reveal important personal constructs they had not previously articulated to their spouses.

However, the concept of an interpersonal dimension defined as intimacy continues to have heuristic value. Couples and families who seek therapy are more likely to evaluate the quality of their relationship in terms of closeness rather than in terms of self-disclosure or personal constructs.

INDICATIONS AND CONTRAINDICATIONS

This therapy is indicated for couples who have failed to develop intimacy, failed to sustain intimacy, or are drifting apart. The couple may present because of loss of closeness, persistent arguments, poor communication, lack of affection, lack of commitment, or sexual dysfunction, but if they accept that intimacy is a problem and they are willing to participate in sessions of mutual self-disclosure, they will benefit from this approach.

The foregoing definition would be an ideal couple for any counseling as they recognize and accept responsibility for an interpersonal difficulty. They would probably benefit from any approach, but they seem particularly suited to a therapy which directly addresses their perceived difficulty. Couples like this represent about 10% of my outpatient referrals and are an important source of therapist satisfaction.

This approach is indicated for families with behavior disorders of childhood or adolescence if either before or after the assessment the parents accept that deficiencies in the quality and quantity of their intimacy play a role in initiating or sustaining the family dysfunction. The therapy has been used with the parents in families where one of the offspring has schizophrenia. The schizophrenic always has received individual treatment and medication. I have the general impression that in those families where the parents actively participated in therapy which also includes education about schizophrenia and parental support group, the course and outcome of the schizophrenic illness have been more benign than in couples with marital discord who have not wanted to participate. These observations must be interpreted cautiously. The quality of marriage in the parents of schizophrenics may not be different from the quality of marriage in the general population. Families where a child has a psychosomatic illness such as anorexia nervosa have also received treatment with apparent benefit to the course and outcome of the psychosomatic problem.

In families where the parents do not accept that deficiencies of intimacy are directly related to clinical situations like suicide attempts or acting out by the children, but who have somewhat reluctantly initiated therapy, an unusual result often occurs. The behavior of the adolescent improves or the parents become less enmeshed in the problem. While measures of family function improve, measures of marital adjustment worsen. Perhaps more than 10 sessions with the parents would be necessary to see objective evidence of improved intimacy. It would appear that in the process of making covert marital discord overt, the family and the offspring benefit.

Couples often seek marital counseling and attribute discord to some undesirable trait or behavior of the spouse. If they are capable of curiosity about why they would select a person with such an undesirable trait, they will benefit from self-disclosure. If they suggest the trait such as selfishness or behavior such as an explosive temper was not present when they met, but they are willing to explore how it emerged in the couple's interaction, they may benefit from therapy.

I should point out that like any other psychotherapy if each member of the couple is honest, genuinely motivated to understand the relationship, assumes responsibility for his or her contribution to the discord, is psychologically minded and curious about interpersonal relationships, therapy is often both interesting and fun for the couple and the therapist. However, one of the advantages of the self-disclosure technique is that it can also be used with couples who lack any or all of the foregoing characteristics. The only limitations appear to be couples who refuse to self-disclose or who believe their parents' relationships have nothing to do with their current marriage. The therapy has also been used with unmarried but committed couples.

Lest you think I am going to suggest enhancing marital intimacy through facilitating cognitive self-disclosure is indicated for everything, let me discuss some contraindications. This therapy is contraindicated in couples where one or both spouses are currently suffering from a major depressive disorder. Our research has shown that although these severely depressed spouses often attribute their symptoms to an inability to feel close to the spouse, the process of self-disclosure may make them more depressed. The treatment of choice appears to be either antidepressant medication with supportive individual therapy or perhaps the individual cognitive therapy described by Beck (1967). When the depression has improved, if the couple still wish to explore the relationship—although few do—self-disclosure may be indicated but also may contribute to relapse.

Another relative contraindication is where one or both spouses suffer from alcoholism (although a few of my students report they have had some success with this group). A precondition of accepting such couples would be the use of Antabuse, attendance at Alcoholics Anonymous, and a period of several months of abstinence. The strange pattern that I have seen frequently is that the couple does well for four of five sessions. For reasons I do not understand, after five or six sessions of self-disclosure a drinking binge occurs and what has been disclosed explodes into at best arguments and at worst violence. The couple report that they are worse off than at the beginning, demoralized, and threaten to separate or actually separate. One student had a suicide. Obviously this contraindication may be a countertransference problem of my own but without further positive experience by other therapists, results suggest caution.

Therapy is contraindicated with a psychotic spouse because they are unable to self-disclose. The therapy has been useful with married schizophrenics when they are not acutely disturbed.

One final caution is necessary. Self-disclosure places tremendous pressure for spouses to reveal honestly what they think. If you have a patient who you know has a secret which the spouse wishes not to reveal, do not involve him or her in cognitive self-disclosure.

I would like to describe several clinical conditions for which this approach may be the treatment of choice. The first is where one or both spouses have symptoms of nonpsychotic emotional illness which they attribute to marital discord. Symptoms of nonpsychotic emotional illness refer to the psychological and physical expression of morbid anxiety or dysphoria. These disorders used to be described by the terms anxiety neurosis and neurotic depression.

When patients with these symptoms spend most of an assessment interview talking about their marriages or attribute their symptoms to an inability to confide in their spouses or complain of their spouses' refusal to accept the existence of marital discord or refuse to do anything to improve marital maladjustment, a marital assessment is indicated. These interviews usually reveal a pervasive lack of intimacy, including lack of affection, poor sexual functioning, absence of communication, lack of compatibility, and failing commitment. This therapy consistently produces significant and clinically meaningful reduction in symptoms of anxiety and depression.

Patients with psychosomatic symptoms such as hypo-chondriasis, morbid obesity, and chronic pain as well as those with heart disease which has failed to improve with traditional medical approaches also benefit from cognitive self-disclosure. Although these couples often believe they have good marriages because they do not argue and be-cause their spouses support them when they are sick, they have a specific pattern of deficient intimacy.

These couples do not argue because they never disclose what they think about relationships. The couple is always socially isolated; each spouse expresses little affection; and poor sexual relationships are typical. In contrast to the neurotic group, these couples are committed and often compatible. Therapy is indicated for these patients and may have broader indications in psychosomatic medicine than my experience to date suggests.

Cognitive Family Therapy is also indicated for couples with sexual dysfunction if the marital relationship is thought to be initiating or sustaining the sexual problem. My col-leagues in our sexual dysfunction clinic often combine sessions of mutual self-disclosure with education and spe-cific behavioral techniques. Whether this approach would be helpful to couples where one spouse has a paraphilia remains to be seen.

Two other problems where enhancing intimacy through self-disclosure has proven useful is for couples where a spouse has made a suicide attempt or suffers from path-ological jealousy. The suicide attempt is often an expression of rage and frustration at a spouse who will not address issues of marital discord. Pathological jealousy often relates to undisclosed sexual personal constructs which can lead to violence if undisclosed.

The final group encompasses couples where one or both spouses have character defects or personality disorders. Although therapy is indicated to address certain interpersonal issues which surface as marital discord in these couples, it would be ambitious to suggest that this 10-session therapy results in personality change. The self-disclosure rather helps couples to accept traits of character and become less preoccupied with the spouse's mixture of frailties. Combinations that seem to derive the most benefit are the compulsive–hysteric union, the passive–aggressive spouse married to a narcissistic personality, and the dependent–independent pattern. I have no experience with severe personality disorders such as paranoids, schizoids, or borderlines. Psychopaths can pretend to be seeking help with marital therapy, but they usually drop out quickly.

Currently, we have research projects which are objectively evaluating outcome in couples with a dysthymic spouse and parents of schizophrenic offspring. The indications and contraindications for this therapy will be re-evaluated as clinical experience and research broaden.

COMPARISON OF COGNITIVE FAMILY THERAPY TO OTHER APPROACHES

You have by now read sections of this book which may have reminded you of an approach or a specific method of marital or family therapy that you practice or have studied. I now attempt to describe aspects of Cognitive Family Therapy which are similar to or have been influenced by other approaches or methods of marital and family therapy. Although this approach evolved out of clinical experience and empirical research, I am sure that certain elements have both consciously and unconsciously evolved out of other therapists' ideas and practices. The main reason they have not been referred to earlier is that utilizing cognitive self-disclosure is very different from the way I was taught to do therapy and because none of the better known teachers or models provided a specific starting point since, to my knowledge, Erik Erikson was not a family therapist.

The written work of Murray Bowen has probably had the greatest direct influence on the development of therapy starting with his early concept of emotional divorce (Bowen, 1975). In my work with couples and families, I was impressed by how common it was for couples to live in passionless and empty relationships while being preoccupied with their children's distress. The development of an operational definition of deficiencies of marital intimacy may have evolved from the concept of emotional divorce.

Bowen later referred to the tension created by this emotional divorce as resulting in a process of triangulation of an offspring, who becomes a focus to diminish tension while helping the couple avoid dealing with their discord. Bowen went on to describe how such couples can triangulate therapists so that they become emotionally invested in the marital conflict. The therapist notes that some behavior of one or the other spouse is preventing clinical progress. The family problem becomes the therapist's problem and the therapist emotionally reacts to the couple rather than responding to the couple's need to resolve or understand their emotional divorce.

Bowen suggested that the best method for achieving this goal was to reconnect the more anxious spouse with his or her family of origin. The observation that this spouse is emotionally invested in distancing from understanding some painful aspect of his or her experience in the family of origin is very similar to our comments about the development of personal constructs through observation and experience of the parents' level of intimacy. Bowen suggests that as the more anxious spouse differentiates from the family of origin, the factors in the emotional divorce can be resolved. Bowen's therapy is also similar in that he advocates treating the family through sessions with one specific individual who learns to *respond* rather than *react* to the family of origin. While our therapy focuses on one dimension of one interpersonal relation—intimacy in the marriage—our research and therapy could be viewed as an operationalization of many of Bowen's key concepts. The therapeutic use of mutual self-disclosure was developed in part to allow therapists to respond rather than react to emotional divorce.

A second approach which has many obvious similarities to this therapy is Sager's approach to marital therapy involving the exploration of unspoken contracts (Sager, 1976). Sager refers to a number of partner types which are based on verbalized expectations, conscious but unverbalized needs, and contracts which are beyond awareness. Obviously, the conscious but unverbalized expectations can be seen as the focus of self-disclosure of personal constructs. The therapist in Sager's model acts as a facilitator, who attempts to allow the couple to make their needs and expectations explicit. The technique would appear to be similar to our specific focus on self-disclosure as may other techniques such as circular questioning or positive reframing. One wonders whether many apparently different approaches are not similar in technique—the attempt to understand current discord through making unverbalized ideas about relationships which may derive from observed relationships available to both spouses for examination.

Other elements of this therapy would appear to include elements of other approaches. The inclusion of only the parents in the therapy sessions involves a technical strategy which may directly address the issue of enmeshment described in Minuchin's (1970) structural therapy. The focus on only cognitive self-disclosure may make use of a paradox which stimulates feelings between the couple outside the sessions, viewed in the model of strategic therapy.

While the focus of the self-disclosure is the couple's personal constructs about the parents' marriages, many family therapies focus on exploration of the family of origin whether directly by having sessions with the couple and their parents, by encouraging the spouses to visit their parents outside of sessions, or by exploring their feelings, attitudes, or memories of their parents.

Finally, if one views the therapy as simply focusing on one aspect of a couple's communication pattern—self-disclosure—the therapy is similar to many types of marital counseling which focus on communication.

It is somewhat easier to describe the family and marital approaches which this therapy does not resemble. The first is approaches that encourage expression of feelings, the second is approaches that focus on interaction in the here and now, the third is approaches that give specific advice, exercises, or tasks, and the fourth is approaches that utilize the therapist's experience or intuition to tell the couple or family something which they may not be fully aware of or have perceived. Because of the brief nature of the sessions, this therapy does not explicitly focus on unconscious motivation.

Rather than describing the specific therapists and theorists who have advocated these approaches, I will make several comments about these differences.

Assisting patients to experience and express their feelings is one of the most cherished values in the mental health professions. In individual therapy the ability to disclose in an emotionally charged, confiding relationship is a widely accepted cornerstone of the helping relationship. I suggest that in work with couples the expression of feeling may interfere with disclosure by the use of tears or anger to avoid responding to disclosures. This opinion is by no means proven and studies of affective versus cognitive self-disclosure may resolve this issue.

Family therapy and marital therapy have often been approached from the gestalt posture of observing and identifying patterns of nonverbal communication, inter-personal patterns of interaction, or techniques of role playing. These approaches are dramatic and stimulating to observe and to practice. Although they may also be effective, they are clearly unacceptable to some clients and unless a clear treatment contract is established they may lead to a high dropout rate. These observations may be applicable to therapy conducted by gifted and intuitive therapists. Cognitive Family Therapy was designed in part as a technique which therapists without unique and charismatic qualities might utilize. The behavioral approaches which focus on specific aspects of behavioral reinforcement have proven successful, but specific homework in this therapy has not proven to be necessary. We do encourage couples who cannot answer specific questions about their families to attempt to obtain the information if possible.

GENERAL PSYCHOTHERAPY ISSUES

Psychotherapists generally agree that there are factors in all psychotherapeutic approaches independent of the specific techniques employed. These factors include 1) non-specific relationship factors; 2) contract setting; 3) placebo factors; 4) transference; 5) countertransference; 6) resistances; and 7) factors outside of therapy.

Nonspecific Relationship Factors

Jerome Frank (1974) has identified factors common to all helping relationships. These include restoration of morale, provision of hope, a shared world view between client and helper, disclosure, emotionally charged atmosphere, and structure. This therapy demonstrates most of these elements so that it is an open question whether effectiveness is a result of the process of self-disclosure, self-awareness which develops through self-disclosure, or general factors such as the couple's decision to seek help and complete therapy.

One example emerges from our research on severely or moderately depressed married women. In these studies the women either receive antidepressants or a placebo in combination with supportive therapy or cognitive self-disclosure. Almost all women in these studies are significantly less depressed at 10 weeks, independent of which group they are randomly assigned to including the combination of placebo and supportive care, the so-called control condition. While further research may demonstrate the drug–self-disclosure combination is superior, one must account for the control group experience. Among general factors which have emerged is the fact that couples who agree to participate in the research may be different from those who refuse. That these women's husbands are willing to come for an assessment and actively participate in 10 therapy sessions suggests that these husbands are different from the spouses of many depressed women who refuse to be interviewed. Research suggests that spouse participation in any therapy program is a potent general factor.

To return to the elements which Frank has identified, enhancing marital intimacy offers hope to despairing couples and families that through learning a new way of listening to one another they can hope to reduce discord in their marriage and family. The belief system that intimacy is valued and influenced by experience in the family of origin is the world view shared by family and therapist. The disclosure in the emotionally charged atmosphere of the marital discord is unique to this therapy in that the disclosure is made actively to the therapist's questions but also passively to one's spouse. Cognitive self-disclosure could hardly be more structured from assessment interview to questionnaires, to explaining the theory, to the specific sessions, and finally to the structured feedback. This approach would appear to maximize many of the nonspecific therapeutic factors common to all effective psychotherapies and helping relationships.

Contract Setting

Recently increased attention has been paid to the importance of obtaining informed, voluntary consent for all treatment from competent clients. Contract setting addresses some of these issues by making explicit what the therapist will do, what is expected of the couple, what will be done in the sessions, and what the potential consequences will be, good or bad.

"Come back next week and we will talk some more about your problems." A common phrase in the mental health profession, but hardly a treatment contract! Cognitive self-disclosure has the advantage of allowing couples a truly informed consent. The theoretical basis of the technique is explained, what will happen in the sessions can be demonstrated as well as explained, and the potential outcome and possible side effects can be described. The specificity and explicitness of the treatment allow the couple to recognize when students deviate from the expected treatment and allow the therapist to easily identify resistance, transference, and lack of honest motivation.

The explicit nature of the treatment contract allows couples to address common concerns about therapy. One is whether the therapist will advise separation or divorce. The couple is told such decisions are theirs, but that it will be a more informed choice after 10 sessions. Couples are told that if one or both spouses persistently interrupt, the session will be terminated.

Clinical experience suggests that the explicit treatment contract allows couples to concentrate on their own relationship rather than focusing their attention on what is expected by the therapist. Couples who do not accept the theory of personal constructs or who do not want to participate in mutual self-disclosure can plan some other form of counseling.

Placebo Factors

A placebo is an inert chemical substance which looks like and is taken as if it were an active drug. The analogy for enhancing marital intimacy would be a therapist who looks like he or she is facilitating cognitive self-disclosure of personal constructs. Although the analogy is not strictly valid and we do not use placebos of this therapy clinically, in research we have used control groups which provide insight into factors that may operate in therapy.

The first was mentioned earlier when we suggested that just the willingness of couples to sit in the same room together for an hour may be more time together than most couples spend at home in a week. Second, the fact that they interact without argument or criticism may have beneficial effects. Third, the couple's completion of questionnaires with feedback and discussion may have therapeutic value on its own. The couple may travel together to the sessions or have dinner afterward where they discuss the sessions, the therapist, or the content.

The therapist is also modeling a different way of communicating which involves active listening and interpersonal curiosity. Couples may copy or imitate this pattern of questioning and listening.

Transference

Transference is a term taken from psychoanalysis which refers to unconscious feelings, thoughts, and impulses transferred from important people in the past to the therapist. Transference can be positive or negative. Whether transference from two spouses to a therapist in 10 sessions is a significant factor is debatable but should not be ignored. Generally, in individual therapy negative transference can produce a resistance to understanding. For example, a patient may feel angry at a therapist for being late for an appointment. This anger may motivate a prolonged silence, which prevents understanding.

This approach may maximize positive transference, which may produce almost magical expectations. The therapist is viewed as an expert who knows what causes discord and how to improve the couples' relationship. The ability to structure interviews, suppress negative feelings, and control behavior may give the couple the impression of a benign but powerful figure.

Negative transference can be more problematic as one or both spouses may experience feelings of anger or disappointment about the therapist's behavior, appearance, interpersonal style, or personality. These feelings need ventilation and may be related to feelings about parents who were felt to be cold, aloof, or overly rational. The therapist must be aware that these emotional reactions often occur during therapy when the couple are close to disclosing personal constructs which may be the specific focus of discord.

These transferences often involve behaviors which suggest that in spite of the therapeutic contract to self-disclose the couple appear to expect the therapist to judge who is right and who is wrong, give specific advice, or advocate one spouse's point of view.

Countertransference

This term refers to the feelings, thoughts, and impulses which the therapist develops toward the couple. Cognitive Family Therapy was specifically developed to prevent therapists from reacting to couples rather than responding with understanding.

Therapists commonly say this couple would be getting better if only one or the other spouse was not so dishonest or selfish. This is an example of being enmeshed or triangulated because it is the therapist who is feeling frustrated rather than the couple understanding their conflict over the issue of selfishness or honesty. The therapist who responds to marital discord by focusing on enhancing intimacy through facilitating self-disclosure of personal constructs will not feel tired or frustrated at the end of the day by assuming responsibility for traits and behavior which are beyond his or her control.

Resistance

Resistance is another term borrowed from psychoanalysis which refers to the unconscious resistance to free association in spite of a conscious agreement to participate in this technique. This concept is probably more appropriately applied to cognitive self-disclosure. Couples show resistance to self-disclosure in spite of a conscious agreement to participate.

The therapist should note when spouses say they were not thinking anything or when a spouse interrupts or behaves in a disruptive way. The spouse should be made aware of the therapy agreement, but the content should be focused on because the spouse has reacted rather than responded to a critical personal construct.

One should remember that spouses have an emotional investment in not understanding their own motives, which may be less than desirable.

Factors Outside Therapy

In a couple's life cycle, belief that 10 hours in a therapist's office is the only factor that predicts a couple's closeness would be foolish. I have had couples who attribute their improved relationships to becoming born-again Christians, prolonged separations, life-threatening circumstances, sexual flings, and criminal charges. All these examples appear to have in common shifts of attitudes regarding the importance of their relationships in response to external threats.

Another factor is that individuals may change habits, traits, or behaviors which have been a focus of dispute for reasons other than pleasing the spouse.

Finally, couples' expectations of marriage may change dramatically over the family life cycle. Time continues to play an important role in closeness in relationships.

HOW DOES SELF-DISCLOSURE ENHANCE INTIMACY?

I next describe several possible explanations of how the technique of facilitating self-disclosure enhances intimacy: 1) through increasing the amount of self-disclosure; 2) through ensuring the reciprocity of self-disclosure; 3) through focusing on the ego-relevance of disclosures; and 4) through increasing the ability of spouses to respond rather than react to self-disclosure.

Increasing the Amount of Self-Disclosure Between Spouses

Increasing the amount of self-disclosure by each spouse in a marriage would be expected to increase the amount of intimacy. Some empirical support for this comes from the finding that a significant, positive, and linear combination of the quantitative aspects of self-disclosing behavior can account for almost half the variance in the ratings of a couple's level of intimacy. Thus, although self-disclosure and intimacy cannot be considered synonymous, the process of self-disclosure is a major determinant of a couple's perception of intimacy. A relationship between the amount of self-disclosure and marital adjustment has been demonstrated (Davidson, Blaswick, & Halverson, 1983).

Some general limitations to the process of increasing the amount of self-disclosure between spouses should be made explicit. A spouse revealing that he or she is having an affair is in my view not self-disclosing but self-exposing. This self-exposing behavior will usually produce distance and not closeness. Self-disclosure would involve revealing the motivations for the dissatisfactions which might lead to an affair.

A spouse who uses the opportunity of an assessment interview to say that he or she has never really loved his or her spouse is not engaging in self-disclosure. This behavior is simply dishonesty. If the spouse was willing to disclose the motivations for the dishonesty or why he or she would marry someone not cared for in the first place, self-disclosure would be occurring.

Does too much self-disclosure harm a relationship (Cozby, 1973)? I believe self-exposure and dishonesty are extremely common in couples with marital problems and do prevent intimacy. For example, if a couple marry because the woman is pregnant, but after the wedding she reveals that she lied about the pregnancy, this can hardly be considered honest self-disclosure.

There are several aspects of the amount of self-disclosure which should be clarified. Usually, the more a spouse becomes involved in self-disclosure, the more personal and private the disclosures become, and the degree of exploration of the psychological motivations for spouse selection become more sophisticated. The disclosures must also be affectively congruent, which means a kind of psychological and interpersonal honesty. If a spouse says that he or she supports the mate's growing independence, the spouse should both act supportive and not speak in a sarcastic tone. Often spouses may not be able to disclose motivations or needs because the reasons are beyond their awareness (i.e., unconscious), or they have not asked themselves or thought about the reasons for a behavior. Finally, not all disclosures may be constructive. Our results clearly indicate that negative self-statements are related inversely to intimacy (Chelune et al., 1984a&b). Spouses who repeatedly state they are worthless may produce distance. Marital therapists may be well advised not to encourage couples to merely "let it all hang out." Self-disclosure of negative self-concepts and negative feelings such as criticism will not increase intimacy.

In summary, increasing the amount of self-disclosure between spouses can be expected to increase intimacy if the disclosures are positive or neutral in both feeling and content, are honest, and are not exposing secrets.

The process of self-disclosure occurs from the first time a couple meet, through courtship, and throughout marriage. Attraction to the opposite-sex person is usually related to issues of physical attraction, reputation, and situational factors. But as the individuals get to know one another, they reveal attitudes and values about children, sexuality, power, and religion which facilitate closeness if similar. Couples with marital problems often deny the importance of disclosing these values and attitudes, believing that love and/or marriage will somehow almost magically prevent conflicts about these issues. However, when children need to go to church or decisions about contraception are pressing, these issues become the focus for dispute. Self-disclosure must explore why these incompatibilities were minimized during courtship and may facilitate closeness by allowing couples to recognize compatibilities.

Examples may help the reader understand what increasing the amount of self-disclosure really means. A spouse may seek counseling because she believes her husband is selfish. Self-disclosure would involve her attempts to explain why she selected or stays married to a selfish person. A husband may want help with his frustration that his wife is not interested in sex. His self-disclosure might involve exploring why sexual refusal makes him so angry or why he selected an asexual person or what he is doing to turn his wife off sex. A couple who say they cannot communicate may use self-disclosure to explore why they are giving a clear message that they have nothing to talk about.

Reciprocity of Self-Disclosure

A variety of studies on interpersonal relationships in marriage have emphasized that marital adjustment is related to a factor referred to variously as "compatibility," "homogamy," "reciprocity," "equity," or "collusion" (Burgess, 1981; Hatfield & Walster, 1981; Murstein, 1974; Willi, 1982). The authors of these studies have identified that similarity of unconscious motivation, personality, attitudes, values, social factors, and even physical appearance and size predict marital adjustment. This suggests that to facilitate intimacy, self-disclosure should be reciprocal.

Social exchange theory suggests that a balance in the amount of self-disclosure between partners will predict greater intimacy (Levinger & Senn, 1967). According to social exchange theory, we consciously review the costs and the rewards of our relationships and if the rewards outweigh the costs, the relationship will continue. A spouse may believe that the mate is selfish and demanding but also attractive and a good companion and as a result tolerate the costs to maintain the rewards.

Psychodynamic therapists believe social exchange theory is simplistic and denies the importance of unconscious motivation in spouse selection and sustaining marital discord (Lidz, 1968; Martin, 1976). As evidence they point to the type of relationships in which costs obviously outweigh rewards, but the couple wish to continue the relationship for unconscious neurotic reasons. This observation may be an example of reciprocity or equity operating at the unconscious level.

Willi (1982) suggests unconscious equity in that many couples have an unconscious collusion to remain at the same level of emotional immaturity. Dominion (1979) has reviewed data which suggest that couples are compatible for neuroticism. It is possible that couples with good adjustment show "conscious'" equity, whereas couples with poor adjustment show "unconscious" equity. Neurotic individuals may avoid self-disclosure because of a fear that they may reveal incompatibilities or inequities. Facilitating self-disclosure may facilitate intimacy in these marriages by revealing equity or compatibility for specific insecurities.

In summary, theories from psychodynamic psychology, developmental psychology, social psychology, and interpersonal psychology suggest that reciprocity and equity are characteristics which promote compatibility and homogamy. Self-disclosure between spouses should be reciprocal in amount, privacy, time, and content to maximize the therapeutic potential of this technique.

Ego Relevance of Disclosures

Couples with marital discord could disclose their attitudes about nuclear war, politics, or religion. This disclosure
might increase their intimacy, but most couples would
consider these topics irrelevant to their discord. Fortunately,
most couples who perceive deficiencies in their level of
closeness seem to accept that the quality of the interpersonal relationships between their grandparents, parents,
siblings, and peers prior to their marriage may be relevant
to their current discord. For example, a couple who present
for therapy with a power conflict will often reveal that
their parents also had problems resolving conflicts. Often
they will blame one parent for these arguments initially,
but self-disclosure may help them identify behaviors in
the other parent which sustained the arguments and also
operate in their own marriage. There are of course a few
couples who do not accept the relevance of these relationships and this type of therapy is not indicated for
these couples.

Psychodynamic theories suggest the quality of attachment between infant and mother lays the groundwork for
the development of intimacy in adulthood (Bowlby, 1958).
While there is no doubt considerable psychological truth
to this hypothesis, couples are unable to disclose verbally
the quality of these relationships before the age of 3. They
may, however, be able to report what they have been told
about the relationships by others.

What appears to be more relevant to the development
of intimacy in adulthood is the child's observation and
experience of the parents' marriage between the ages of
about 4 to 15. The child observes how his or her parents
express affection, how they resolve differences of opinion,

how they relate to in-laws and other couples, how they spend their leisure time, and how they communicate with one another. The child also experiences feelings of insecurity regarding the marriage when there is tension between the parents regarding commitment, sexuality, or difficulties with alcoholism, affairs, or physical or verbal abuse. Spouses in therapy with marital problems often report that their own insecurity in their childhood is due to a personal construct about one of the parents who they believed caused their parents' marital discord or disruption. They often report that they have made conscious decisions not to repeat patterns they observed in their parents' marriages. Couples also believe that relationships with grandparents, siblings, and peers have influenced their attitudes and beliefs about relationships with the opposite sex. Experience with self-disclosure to siblings, best friends, and relatives of thoughts which they believe they cannot reveal to parents is also important.

Finally, exploration of the motives which attracted individuals to their spouses and led to the decision to marry are also relevant to understanding their problems with intimacy. In summary, self-disclosure of information about couples' observations of their parents' relationships and the couples' own motives ensures the relevance of the content and often provides illuminating insights.

Responding Versus Reacting to Self-Disclosure

Bowen (1975) suggested that couples who cannot resolve interpersonal conflict will involve a third party (including a therapist) to reduce tension, but will also avoid resolving the issue. Spouses often respond emotionally (usually tears or anger) to disclosures that they do not wish to hear. Self-disclosure must be responded to through empathic listening in order to promote intimacy. Couples often have personal constructs or beliefs which they are reluctant to give up. The therapist must ensure that the spouse appears to be listening. A fundamental rule of self-disclosure therapy is that a spouse may not interrupt while the other spouse is disclosing. The therapist must be aware that when a spouse attempts to break this rule, the spouse is reacting to a primary conflict which is always an impasse for developing intimacy. When a therapist feels that therapy is *not* progressing because of the characteristics of *one* spouse, that therapist is also reacting and not responding to the other spouse's contribution to the difficulty with intimacy.

Assuming that future research demonstrates that this technique is effective, what does the therapy tell us about self-disclosure in marriage? Does the process of self-disclosure facilitate intimacy independent of type or content of disclosures? Does the couple learn through modeling, a type of communication which has been lacking in their relationship? Does cognitive restructuring of undisclosed schemas facilitate change? Does preventing the couple from speaking directly for 10 one-hour sessions produce a paradoxical increase in conversation outside the sessions? Are nonspecific psychotherapy factors such as restoration of morale by preventing arguments or encouraging interpersonal curiosity operating? These questions must remain unanswered until studies which vary technique, type of disclosure, content of disclosure, and other therapy and therapist components and correlate them with specific outcome measures are completed.

Clinical experience from couples who have participated and therapists who have been trained to use the technique have generated some hypotheses. The majority of couples say that they have never communicated in both the style and about the content of self-disclosure in the time that they have been married. Obviously, they are learning a novel way of communicating about relationships.

Couples rarely report learning or revealing some specific cognitive schema which has changed their feelings or attitudes. Perhaps more than 10 sessions would be necessary for this type of cognitive restructuring to occur. However, they report a greater understanding of their spouse and often to their surprise their relationship has improved without their doing anything specific. Couples report that greater understanding and improved communication make them feel closer. In support of the hypothesis that it is the process of cognitive self-disclosure rather than content, couples also often tell me that I haven't done very much, but the relationship has improved anyway!

Some preliminary comments about clinical experience with facilitating cognitive self-disclosure and its effect on intimacy are possible. Couples who both objectively and subjectively derive the greatest benefit spend more time disclosing about the past than the present, and about their parents' marriages rather than about their own. The greater the understanding of their own responsibility for mate selection of a spouse with certain qualities or traits (which decreases the amount of projection onto the spouse), the greater the improvement in measures of marital quality. The greater the other spouse can facilitate cognitive restructuring with objective data about his or her own parents' relationship, the greater the improvement in marital intimacy.

The couples articulate that understanding their spouse, learning to be better listeners without reacting defensively or emotionally, and learning about their parents play a role in improving their closeness. The ability to enjoy listening to their parents describe their own marriage is the greatest single predictor of positive outcome.

Finally, the technique has impressed on this observer that the experience and observation of one's parents' level of intimacy has a more obvious influence on developing a parallel repetitive pattern in the current marital relationship than the quality of the affectionate bond between the child and either parent (Waring, 1981). In fact, the spouse in a maladjusted marriage would appear to be acting as "a misguided marital counselor," emotionally reacting and attempting to change behaviors in his or her spouse, which on examination turn out to be the behaviors of the parent who was perceived to be the cause of the parents' lack of intimacy.

THERAPIST FACTORS

One would expect that Cognitive Family Therapy was developed by a therapist who enjoys thinking but avoids feelings and lacks intuition! While this description may or may not be accurate as a description of my clinical style and personal characteristics, Cognitive Family Therapy was developed in part as a technique which would be useful for experienced and inexperienced as well as gifted and ordinary therapists.

My own training involved approaches which were interactional and focused on feelings and motivations. Although I still enjoy this approach, I found it was less effective with couples and often caused much distress for families.

However, therapists are the people who assist couples and families, and various studies have shown that therapists' styles, personal characteristics, attitudes, and experience do influence therapeutic outcome. I will attempt to outline some therapist variables which do seem to influence the success professionals experience with using this approach and technique.

Inexperienced therapists seem to do better with enhancing marital intimacy than do experienced therapists, at least initially. There may be several reasons for this observation. Inexperienced therapists feel considerable uncertainty when they first work with couples and families. This approach gives them a structure for interviewing and therapy. They gain experience while following consistent behavioral patterns rather than through trial and error. Inexperienced therapists have difficulty initially listening to content while also learning to do something about process. This therapy allows the therapist to focus on content as the process is handled in a structured manner.

Experienced therapists often find several features of the self-disclosure approach difficult. First, they have previously learned an approach which may have valued expression of feeling, interventions with process and interaction, and making observations about the couple or family. They often find the cognitive model, the structured format, and the absence of intuitive interventions difficult. Experienced therapists also tend to be eclectic, doing different interventions at different times. They find the structure inhibiting. Most experienced therapists who have learned this technique tend to use self-disclosure at different times with different clients. The hardest part for these therapists is ignoring feelings and allowing the couple to discover where self-disclosure will lead rather than getting ahead of the couple.

Cognitive Family Therapy obviously appeals to therapists whose style is reflective and who are good listeners. The technique is also appealing to individuals who like to be in control and who tend to suppress or avoid feeling.

In summary, although this approach is more appealing to inexperienced, cognitively oriented listeners, I have seen enough therapists with different styles, personalities, and orientations derive benefit to suggest the therapy is not totally dependent on therapist characteristics.

TRAINING

This therapy is learned by teaching the general principles of interviewing couples and families first. The structured approach to gathering information is taught second. Next, the student will sit in with an experienced therapist for 10 sessions of self-disclosure therapy. Next, the student will share 10 sessions with an experienced therapist by providing the self-disclosure for one spouse. After this, supervision is done by listening to audiotapes primarily to ensure that self-disclosure is facilitated and secondarily to improve listening skills.

What I have described is how we train therapists for our research projects. I will describe how readers of this book can train themselves since they do not have the luxury of sitting in for 10 sessions with an experienced therapist.

The first exercise is to use the headings in Chapter 3 to practice interviewing with couples and families.

The second exercise is to write down a summary of each spouse's answers to your cognitive questions. After sessions you can review your material and should notice a ladder of ideas which become more and more specific and provide more information about the family of origin. If there is no new information from session to session, then self-disclosure is not being facilitated.

The third exercise, if you believe the therapy is not progressing, is to audiotape the session and send it to me and I will offer some comments. That is the least I can do for someone who has read my book and wants to try Cognitive Family Therapy.

SUMMARY

I have suggested that couples and families with discord all have problems with intimacy in the marriage. These problems originate in the spouse's personal constructs about relationships observed and experienced in the family of origin. Facilitating self-disclosure between spouses allows the couple to become aware of beliefs which may be the basis of their discord. I believe this approach and technique is both efficient and humane. My major objective now is our continuing research, which will demonstrate effectiveness and narrow the indications. My hope is that this effort will stimulate others to do the same. I hope this book has given you "food for thought."

Appendix

DEFINITION OF TERMS

Affection: The expression of feelings of liking and loving and positive opinions about the spouse.

Autonomy: The couple's relationship to interpersonal relationships outside the marriage including parents, children, and friends, and the quality of these relationships.

Cohesion: The expression of commitment to the marriage and the primacy of the marital relationship.

Compatibility: The sharing of background, attitudes, activities, and goals.

Conflict Resolution: The capacity to resolve differences of opinion without argument, criticism, or refusal to resolve issues.

Expressiveness: The sharing of private thoughts, beliefs, and attitudes as well as feelings and the capacity to communicate about the relationship.

Identity: The couple's opinions about themselves compared to other couples.

Sexuality: A mutually satisfactory expression of sexuality.

References

Ackerman, N. W. *The psychodynamics of family life.* New York: Basic Books, 1958.

Allport, G. W. *Becoming: Basic considerations for a psychology of personality.* New Haven: Yale University Press, 1955.

Aneschenel, C. S., & Stone, J. D. Stress and depression. *Archives of General Psychiatry,* 1982, *39,* 1392–1396.

Beck, A. T. *Depression: Clinical, experimental and therapeutic aspects.* New York: Harper & Row, 1967.

Beck, A. T., Ward, C. H., Mendelson, M., Mock, J., & Erbaugh, J. An inventory for measuring depression. *Archives of General Psychiatry,* 1961, *4,* 561–571.

Beck, D. F. Marital conflict: Its course and treatment as seen by caseworkers. *Social Casework,* 1966, *47,* 211–221.

Beck, D. F. *The treatment of marital problems.* New York: Family Service Association of America, 1970.

Berman, E. M., & Lief, H. I. Marital therapy from a psychiatric perspective: An overview. *American Journal of Psychiatry,* 1975, *132,* 583–592.

Birtchnell, J., & Kennard, J. Marriage and mental illness. *British Journal of Psychiatry,* 1983, *142,* 193–198.

Boszormenyi-Nagy, I., & Framo, J. *Intensive family therapy.* New York: Harper & Row, 1965.

Bowen, M. A. Family concept of schizophrenia. In D. Jackson (Ed.), *The etiology of schizophrenia.* New York: Basic Books, 1960.

Bowen, M. Family therapy after twenty years. In S. Arieti (Ed.), *American handbook of psychiatry*, Volume 5. New York: Basic Books, 1975.

Bowen, M., Dysinger, R. H., & Basamania, B. The role of the father in families with a schizophrenic patient. *American Journal of Psychiatry*, 1959, *115*, 1017–1020.

Bowlby, J. The nature of the child's tie to his mother. *International Journal of Psychoanalysis*, 1958, *39*, 350–372.

Bowlby, J. The role of childhood experience in cognitive disturbance. In M. J. Mahoney & A. Freeman (Eds.), *Cognition and psychotherapy*. New York: Plenum, 1985.

Brown, G. W., Brolchain, M. D., & Harris, T. Social class and psychiatric disturbance among women in an urban population. *Sociology*, 1975, *9*, 225–254.

Brown, G. W., & Harris, T. *Social origins of depression: A study of psychiatric disorder in women*. London: Free Press, 1978.

Burgess, R. L. Relationships in marriage and the family. In S. Duck & R. Gilmour (Eds.), *Personal relationships*, Volume 1. New York: Academic Press, 1981.

Burke, R. J., Weir, T., & Duwors, R. E. Jr. Type A behavior in administrators and wives: Report of marital satisfaction and well-being. *Journal of Applied Psychology*, 1979, *64*(1), 57–65.

Chelune, G. J. Nature and assessment of self-disclosing behavior. In P. McReynolds (Ed.), *Advances in psychological assessment*, Volume 4. San Francisco: Jossey-Bass, 1978.

Chelune, G. J., Sultan, F. E., Vosk, B. N., Ogden, J. K., & Waring, E. M. Self-disclosure patterns in clinical and nonclinical couples. *Journal of Clinical Psychology*, 1984a, *40*(1), 213–215.

Chelune, G. J., Waring, E. M., Vosk, B. N., Sultan, F. E., & Ogden, J. K. Self-disclosure and its relationship to marital intimacy. *Journal of Clinical Psychology*, 1984b, *40*(1), 216–219.

Cozby, P. C. Self-disclosure: A literature review. *Psychological Bulletin*, 1973, *79*(2), 73–91.

Crowe, M. J. Conjoint marital therapy: A controlled outcome study. *Psychological Medicine*, 1978, *8*(4), 623–636.

Davidson, B., Blaswick, J., & Halverson, C. Affective self-disclosure and marital adjustment: A test of equity theory. *Journal of Marriage and the Family*, 1983, *45*(1), 93–102.

Dominion, J. Definition and extent of marital pathology. *British Medical Journal*, 1979, *2*, 478–479.

Erikson, E. H. *Childhood and society*, 2nd ed. New York: Norton, 1950.

Feldman, L. B. Marital conflict and marital intimacy: An integrative psychodynamic behavioral model. *Family Process*, 1979, *18*(1), 69–78.

Frank, J. *Persuasion and healing.* New York: Schocken Books, 1974.

Fredin, L. *Psychological aspects of depression.* New York: Wiley, 1982.

Friedman, A. S. Interaction of drug therapy with marital therapy in depressive patients. *Archives of General Psychiatry,* 1975, *32,* 619–638.

Fromm, E. *The sane society.* New York: Holt, Rinehart & Winston, 1955.

Goldberg, D. P. *Detection of psychiatric illness by questionnaire.* Oxford: Oxford University Press, Maudsley Monograph, 1972.

Greenberg, L. S., & Safran, J. D. Hot cognition—emotion coming in from the cold: A reply to Rachman and Mahoney. *Cognitive Therapy and Research,* 1984, *8*(6), 591–598.

Grinker, R. R. *Toward a unified theory of human behavior,* 2nd ed. New York: Basic Books, 1967.

Gurman, A. S. The effects and effectiveness of marital therapy: A review of outcome research. *Family Process,* 1973, *12,* 145–170.

Gurman, A. S., & Kniskern, D. P. Research on marital and family therapy: Progress, perspective, prospect. In S. L. Garfield & A. E. Bergin (Eds.), *Handbook of psychotherapy and behavior change: An empirical analysis,* 2nd ed. New York: Wiley, 1975.

Haley, J. *Strategies of psychotherapy.* New York: Grune & Stratton, 1963.

Hames, J., & Waring, E. M. Marital intimacy and non-psychotic emotional illness. *Psychiatric Forum,* 1979, *9*(1), 13–19.

Hamilton, M. The assessment of anxiety states by rating. *British Journal of Medical Psychology,* 1959, *32,* 50–55.

Hamilton, M. A rating scale for depression. *Journal of Neurology, Neurosurgery, and Psychiatry,* 1960, *23,* 36–62.

Hatfield, E., & Walster, G. W. *A new look at love.* Reading, MA: Addison-Wesley, 1981.

Henderson, S. The social network, support and neurosis. *British Journal of Psychiatry,* 1977, *131,* 185–197.

Henderson, S. A development in social psychiatry—The systematic study of social bonds. *Journal of Nervous and Mental Disease,* 1980, *168*(2), 63–69.

Henderson, S., Byrne, D. G., Duncan-Jones, P., Scott, R., & Adcock, S. Social relationships, adversity, and neurosis. *British Journal of Psychiatry,* 1980, *136,* 574–583.

Hinde, R. A. Interpersonal relationships—In quest of a science. *Psychological Medicine,* 1978, *3,* 378–386.

Horowitz, L. M. Cognitive structure of interpersonal problems treated in psychotherapy. *Journal of Consulting and Clinical Psychology,* 1979, *47*(1), 5–15.

218 ENHANCING MARITAL INTIMACY

Jackson, D. A sequential system for personality scale development. In C. D. Speilberger (Ed.), *Current topics in clinical and community psychology.* New York: Academic Press, 1970.

Jacob, T. Family interaction in disturbed and normal families: A methodological and substantive review. *Psychological Bulletin,* 1975, *82,* 33–65.

Jacobson, N. S. A review of the research on the effectiveness of marital therapy. In T. J. Paolino & B. S. McCrady (Eds.), *Marriage and marital therapy: Psychoanalytic, behavioral and systems theory perspectives.* New York: Brunner/Mazel, 1978.

Johnson, S. M. A comparative treatment study of experimental and behavioral approaches to marital therapy. Ph.D. Dissertation, University of British Columbia, 1984.

Jourard, S. M. *The transparent self,* rev. ed. New York: Van Nostrand Reinhold, 1971.

Jourard, S. M., & Sasoko, D. Some factors in self-disclosure. *Journal of Abnormal and Social Psychiatry,* 1958, *56,* 91–98.

Jung, C. G. *Memories, dreams, reflections.* New York: Random House, 1961.

Jung, C. G. *Psychological types.* Princeton, NJ: Princeton University Press, Bollingen Series 20, 1971.

Kelly, G. A. *The psychology of personal constructs.* New York: Norton, 1955.

Kreitman, N., Collins, J., Nelson, B., & Troop, J. Neurosis and marital interaction: IV. Manifest psychological interaction. *British Journal of Psychiatry,* 1971, *119,* 243–252.

Kubie, L. The nature of the neurotic process. In S. Arieti (Ed.), *The American handbook of psychiatry,* Volume 3. New York: Basic Books, 1974.

Leff, J. Schizophrenia and sensitivity to the family environment. In R. Cancro (Ed.), *Annual review of the schizophrenic syndrome.* New York: Brunner/Mazel, 1978.

Levinger, G., & Senn, D. J. Disclosure of feelings in marriage. *Merrill Palmer Quarterly,* 1967, *13,* 237–249.

Levinger, G., & Snoek, J. D. *Attraction in relationship: A new look at interpersonal attraction.* Morristown, NJ: General Learning Press, 1972.

Lewis, J. M., Beavers, W. R., Gossett, J. T., & Phillips, V. A. *No single thread: Psychological health in family systems.* New York: Brunner/Mazel, 1976.

Lewis, R. A. A. A developmental framework for the analysis of premarital dyadic formation. *Family Process,* 1972, *11,* 17–48.

Lidz, T. K. *The person: His development through the life cycle.* New York: Basic Books, 1968.

Locke, H. J., & Wallace, E. M. Short marital adjustment and prediction tests: Their reliability and validity. *Marriage and Family Living,* 1959, *21,* 251–255.

Lorr, M., & McNair, P. An interpersonal behavioral circle. *Journal of Abnormal Social Psychology,* 1963, *67,* 68–75.

MacGregor, R., Ritchie, A., & Serrano, A. *Multiple impact therapy with families.* New York: McGraw-Hill, 1964.

Martin, P. *A marital therapy manual.* New York: Brunner/Mazel, 1976.

Meichenbaum, D. *Cognitive-behavior modification: An integrative approach.* New York: Plenum, 1977.

Merikangas, K. R. Divorce and assortative mating among depressed patients. *American Journal of Psychiatry,* 1984, *141*(1), 74–76.

Minuchin, S. The use of an ecological framework in the treatment of a child. In E. J. Anthony & C. Koupernik (Eds.), *The child in his family* (Vol. 1). New York: Wiley-Interscience, 1970.

Minuchin, S. *Families and family therapy.* Cambridge, MA: Harvard University Press, 1974.

Mitchell, R. E., Cronkite, R. C., & Moos, R. F. Stress, coping and depression among married couples. *Journal of Abnormal Psychology,* 1983, *92,* 433–448.

Moos, R. H., & Moos, B. A typology of family social environments. *Family Process,* 1976, *15,* 357–372.

Murstein, B. I. *Love, sex, and marriage through the ages.* New York: Springer, 1974.

Noller, P. *Nonverbal communication and marital interaction.* Oxford: Pergamon Press, 1984.

Olson, D. H. Marital and family therapy: Integrative review and critique. *Journal of Marriage and the Family,* 1970, *32,* 501–538.

Olson, D. H., Russell, C. S., & Sprenkle, G. H. Circumplex model of marital and family systems: I. Cohesion and adaptability dimensions, family types, and clinical application. *Family Process,* 1979, *18*(1), 3–28.

Pattison, E. M. A theoretical-empirical base for social system therapy. In E. F. Feulks, R. M. Wintrob, J. Westenmayer, & A. R. Favazza (Eds.), *Current perspective in culture and psychiatry.* New York: Spectrum, 1977.

Patton, D., & Waring, E. M. The quality and quantity of marital intimacy in the marriages of psychiatric patients. *Journal of Sex and Marital Therapy,* 1984, *10*(3), 201–206.

Piaget, J. *Structuralism.* New York: Basic Books, 1970.

Quinton, D., Rutter, M., & Rowlands, A. An evaluation of an interview assessment of marriage. *Psychological Medicine*, 1976, *6*, 577–586.

Rachman, S. A reassessment of the "Primacy of Affect." *Cognitive Therapy and Research*, 1984, *8*(6), 579–584.

Reiss, D. Intimacy and problem-solving. *Archives of General Psychiatry*, 1971, *25*, 442–455.

Ruestow, P., Dunner, D., Bleecker, B., & Fieve, R. R. Marital adjustment in primary affective disorder. *Comprehensive Psychiatry*, 1978, *19*, 565–571.

Russell, A., Russell, L., & Waring, E. M. Cognitive family therapy: A preliminary report. *Canadian Journal of Psychiatry*, 1980, *25*, 64–67.

Sager, C. J. *Marriage contracts and couple therapy*. New York: Brunner/ Mazel, 1976.

Satir, V. *Conjoint family therapy*. Palo Alto, CA: Science and Behavior Books, 1967.

Schaefer, M. T., & Olson, D. H. Assessing intimacy: The PAIR inventory. *Journal of Marital and Family Therapy*, 1981, *7*, 47–60.

Schutz, W. *The interpersonal underworld*. Palo Alto, CA: Science and Behavioral Books, 1966.

Segraves, R. T. *Marital therapy*. New York: Plenum, 1982.

Sharan, S. Family interaction with schizophrenics and their siblings. *Journal of Abnormal Psychology*, 1966, *71*, 345–353.

Sifneos, P. Problems of psychotherapy of patients with alexithymic characteristics and physical disease. *Psychotherapy and Psychosomatics*, 1975, *26*(2), 65–70.

Skynner, R., & Cleese, J. *Families and how to survive them*. London: Methuen, 1983.

Speck, R. V., & Rueveni, U. Network therapy—A developing concept. *Family Process*, 1969, *8*, 182–191.

Spitzer, R. L., Endicott, J. E., & Robins, E. Research Diagnostic Criteria: Rationale and reliability. *Archives of General Psychiatry*, 1978, *35*, 773–782.

Strupp, H. H., Hadley, S. W., & Gomes-Schwartz, B. *Psychotherapy for better or worse: The problem of negative effects*. New York: Jason Aronson, 1977.

Sullivan, H. S. *The interpersonal theory of psychiatry*. New York: Norton, 1953.

Tennant, C., Hurry, J., & Bebbington, P. The relation of childhood experience to adult depressive and anxiety states. *British Journal of Psychiatry*, 1982, *141*, 475–482.

Vaillant, G. Natural history of male psychological health: VI. Correlates of successful marriage and fatherhood. *American Journal of Psychiatry*, 1978, *135*(6), 653–659.

Waring, E. M. Family therapy and schizophrenia. *Canadian Psychiatric Association Journal*, 1978, *23*(7), 51–58.

Waring, E. M. Marital intimacy, psychosomatic symptoms, and cognitive therapy. *Psychosomatics*, 1980, *21*(7), 595–601.

Waring, E. M. Facilitating marital intimacy through self-disclosure. *American Journal of Family Therapy*, 1981, *9*(4), 33–42.

Waring, E. M. Marriages of patients with psychosomatic illness. *General Hospital Psychiatry*, 1983, *5*, 49–53.

Waring, E. M. The measurement of marital intimacy. *Journal of Marital and Family Therapy*, 1984, *10*(2), 185–192.

Waring, E. M., & Chelune, G. J. Marital intimacy and self-disclosure. *Journal of Clinical Psychology*, 1983, *39*(2), 183–190.

Waring, E. M., Frelick, L., Tillmann, M. P., Russell, L., & McElrath, D. Marital intimacy and neurosis. *Hillside Journal of Clinical Psychiatry*, 1984, *6*(1), 79–89.

Waring, E. M., McElrath, D., Mitchell, P., & Derry, M. E. Intimacy in the general population. *Canadian Journal of Psychiatry*, 1981a, *26*, 167–172.

Waring, E. M., McElrath, D., Lefcoe, D., & Weisz, G. Dimensions of intimacy in marriage. *Psychiatry*, 1981b, *44*(2), 169–175.

Waring, E. M., & Patton, D. Marital intimacy and depression. *British Journal of Psychiatry*, 1984a, *145*, 641–644.

Waring, E. M., & Patton, D. Marital intimacy and family functioning. *Psychiatric Journal of the University of Ottawa*, 1984b, *9*(1), 24–29.

Waring, E. M., Patton, D., Neron, C. A., & Linker, W. Types of marital intimacy and prevalence of emotional illness. *Canadian Journal of Psychiatry*, 1986, *31*, 720–726.

Waring, E. M., & Reddon, J. R. The measurement of intimacy in marriage: The Waring Intimacy Questionnaire. *Journal of Clinical Psychology*, 1983, *39*, 53–57.

Waring, E. M., Reddon, J. R., Corvinelli, M., Chalmers, W. S., & Vander Laan, R. Marital intimacy and mood states in a nonclinical sample. *Journal of Psychology*, 1983, *115*, 263–273.

Waring, E. M., & Russell, L. Cognitive family therapy. *Journal of Sex and Marital Therapy*, 1980a, *6*(4), 258–273.

Waring, E. M., & Russell, L. Family structure, marital adjustment, and intimacy in patients referred to a consultation-liaison service. *General Hospital Psychiatry*, 1980b, *3*, 198–203.

Waring, E. M., & Russell, L. Cognitive family therapy. In F. W. Kaslow (Ed.), *The international book of family therapy*. New York: Brunner/Mazel, 1982.

Waring, E. M., Tillmann, M. P., Frelick, L., Russell, L., & Weisz, G. Concepts of intimacy in the general population. *Journal of Nervous and Mental Disease*, 1980, *168*(8), 471–474.

Waterman, J. Self-disclosure and family dynamics. In G. Chelune, (Ed.), *The anatomy of self-disclosure.* San Francisco: Jossey-Bass, 1980.

Weissman, M. M., & Paykel, E. K. *The depressed woman: A study of social relationships.* Chicago: University of Chicago Press, 1974.

Wells, R. A., & Dezen, A. E. The results of family therapy revisited: The non-behavioral methods. *Family Process*, 1978, *17*, 251–274.

Wesley, W. A., & Epstein, N. B. *The Silent Majority.* San Francisco: Jossey-Bass, 1969.

Willi, J. *Couples in collusion.* New York: Jason Aronson, 1982.

Winnicott, D. W. *The family and individual development.* London: Tavistock, 1965.

Wynne, L. C., Toohey, M. L., & Doane, J. Family studies. In L. Bellak (Ed.), *Disorders of the schizophrenic syndrome.* New York: Basic Books, 1979.

Zung, W. W. A self-rating depression scale. *Archives of General Psychiatry*, 1963, *12*, 63–70.

Index

223